KIDS EXPLORE AMERICA'S JAPANESE AMERICAN HERITAGE

Westridge Young Writers Workshop

John Muir Publications
Santa Fe, New Mexico

When you read this book you will learn
All kinds of people make the world turn.
Each is different in his or her own way,
We want you to know that that's okay.
These heroes have taught us things we didn't know,
Now along with us you can grow.

John Muir Publications, P.O. Box 613, Santa Fe, NM 87504
© 1994 by Jefferson County School District N. R-1
Cover © 1994 John Muir Publications
Printed in the United States of America

First edition.   First printing March 1994
                    First TWG printing March 1994

Library of Congress Cataloging-in-Publication Data
Kids explore America's Japanese American heritage / Westridge Young
    Writers Workshop. — 1st ed.
    p.   cm.
    Includes index.
    ISBN 1-56261-155-0 : $9.95
    1. Japanese Americans — Juvenile literature. I. Westridge Young Writers Workshop.
E184.J3K454 1994
973' .04956—dc20   93-43567
                                                      CIP
                                                      AC

Design Susan Surprise
Cover Art Tony D'Agostino
Map on page 16 by Jim and Holly Wood
Typefaces Garamond and Helvetica
Printer Malloy Lithographing
Typesetting John Cole

Distributed to the book trade by
W. W. Norton & Co., 500 Fifth Avenue, New York, NY 10110

Distributed to the education trade by
The Wright Group, 19201 120th Avenue NE, Bothell, WA 98011

CONTENTS

ACKNOWLEDGMENTS

We, the 94 student authors, are especially appreciative of the people of Japanese American heritage who shared their time and talent with us. A book like this takes the help of many people. Lots of individuals and groups contributed in preparing the outline, doing research, presenting programs, providing resources, teaching dancing, assisting in the art room, helping with cooking, picking up supplies, or serving in other ways. These are some of the people who made a significant contribution:

Carrie Ann Aoki
Yuri Ariki
Art Arita
Itsu Arita
Tom Beston
Monica Cetuk
Gaylene Endo
Marcia Everson
Jeanne Fagen
Mary Ferguson
Carol Fujioka
Robin Furuta
Eva Hafer
Yoshi Hamamura

Hideo Hamamura
Rev. George Hanabusa
Debbie Harmon
Dr. Lane Hirabayashi
Irene Hirano
Frank Hiraoka
Lorraine Hisamoto
Roy Inouye
Yoshiko Inouye
Craig Iriye
Virgie Ito
Jane Kano
Debbie Kawakami
Kathryn Kawakami
Allison Kochiyama
Tay Kondo
Rev. Eijun Kujo
Sadaharu Kurobane
Kim Manning
D'ann Masaki
Archie Miyatake
Theresa Montoya
Roy Nagai
Kathy Namura
Catherine Nelson
Mary Nishiyama
Nobuko Ninomiya
Sandy Noguchi
Brian Nuija
Rev. Kanya Okamoto

Rose Roy
Ellen Sakamoto
Wes Sakamoto
Janet Sasa
Cindie Shibata
Ruth Shinto
Carol Shito
Pat Stromberg
Mickey Takeshita
Jimmy Tokeshi
Candy Tsutsui
Lillian Uba
Sue Uyeda
Reiko Urano
Aaron Velarde
Arlene Wada
Suzie Weaver
Christine Wanifuchi
Sandy Yamakishi
Ruth Yamauchi
Lulu Yip
Kent Yoritomo

Organizations, churches, temples, and businesses that assisted with presentations, merchandise, or money include the following:

Denver Buddhist Temple
Denver Buddhist Temple Judo Dojo
Denver Central Optimists
Denver Japanese Karate Center and Team
Denver Wholesale Florist
First Bank of South Jeffco
Fort Lupton Japanese American Citizens
    League
Japanese American Curriculum Project
Japanese American Museum
Jr. Denver Taiko Group
Los Angeles Japanese American Citizens
    League
Mums the Word
Pacific Mercantile
Simpson United Methodist Church
U.S. West Foundation
Military Intelligence Veterans Club
Rafu Shimpo newspaper
Sun newspaper
Toyo Miyatake Studios
Tozai Times

TEACHERS' PREFACE

We accept the challenge of building a brighter future. We will not ignore the problems caused by racism in America. We pledge to continue to work for respect for all Americans.

The fourth book in the Kids Explore series, *Kids Explore America's Japanese American Heritage* is a product of the Westridge Young Writers Workshop. The workshop was a ten-day writing project held at Westridge Elementary School in Jefferson County, a western suburb of Denver, Colorado.

Ninety-four students, ages eight to 14, participated in researching, writing, organizing, editing, and illustrating the information that became this book. In addition, 35 teachers and 19 high-school mentors contributed their expertise as they helped the authors learn about history, food, celebrations, the arts, folk tales, and literature, as well as about real people and heroes. The majority of the students and teachers who participated in this project are Japanese American.

Each person in the workshop took part in all the activities, from making artwork, cooking recipes, and watching demonstrations, to learning Japanese words, singing songs, and writing for a section of the book. By participating in all of the activities, the authors developed an appreciation for Japanese American culture as a whole, then shared their knowledge of one aspect of it. The older students wrote the history section. They were able to understand the past and then write about it in a way that young readers can understand. The younger students kept the older authors on track, making sure they used interesting, accessible language.

While the authors worked on enhancing their research and writing skills, the teachers earned graduate college credit through a course titled "Integrating Japanese American Studies into the School Curriculum."

As we learned more about Japanese American heritage, we also explored ways to integrate cultures into school curricula.

One of these ways is through language. This book introduces a number of Japanese words and names, and provides a pronunciation key for all of them. There are five basic vowel sounds in Japanese:

A sounds like "ah," as in "father"
I sounds like "ee," as in "machine"
U sounds like "oo," as in "flu"
E sounds like "eh," as in "get"
O sounds like "oh," as in "hope"

Accented syllables are not used in the Japanese language. Therefore, we do not show a stressed syllable. Syllables are divided after the vowels, with the exception of those ending in "n" or "m." These are the only consonants that can end a syllable (for example, *sen-sei*). All other consonants begin a syllable. Where double consonants occur, syllables are divided between the two, as in *Is-sei*.

During this writing project, we became more aware of the cultural diversity of the United States. In addition, we learned that although people across our country have many different cultural backgrounds, they are all proud to be Americans. In fact, many Japanese Americans who have vacationed in Japan discovered that they are very American indeed, and not Japanese. The diversity of heritage that makes up our country brings a richness to it that blends the past with the present.

As teachers, we have developed a better understanding of diversity, which we can pass on to our students. We have also become more sensitive to and appreciative of Japanese American culture and traditions. It is our hope that this book will contribute to a greater understanding of the many rich cultures in our nation.

HISTORY

Ethnic history should not be ignored,
Read while you learn and pride will be restored.
Remember this chapter about people, struggles, and success,
So you will learn to do your very best.

This section is about Japanese American history—and lots of it! We believe we have written this in a way you can understand. We have included information left out of most children's history books. Japanese Americans are now on a successful path, but to get here they had to face prejudice and discrimination and overcome many challenges.

EARLY JAPANESE IMMIGRATION TO AMERICA

In 1841 in Japan, a man named Manjiro Nakahama (mahn-jee-roh nah-kah-hah-mah) went fishing with four friends. A storm swept their boat to a small island in the North Pacific. Months later, they were rescued by an American sea captain named William Whitfield,

who took them to Hawaii. There they waited for a chance to go back to Japan.

When their chance finally came, Mr. Nakahama decided to stay with Captain Whitfield. Mr. Nakahama learned English and went to school in Massachusetts. About ten years later, Mr. Nakahama went back to Japan to help the Japanese government understand the Americans.

Around 1851, another Japanese boat was stranded at sea. The crew floated for about fifty days on the ocean before they were picked up by an American ship and taken to San Francisco, California. These Japanese sailors were not allowed to go ashore. They had to stay on board the ship for a whole year while plans were made to return them to Japan. It was hard to get the sailors home because Japan had a law at the time that said foreign ships could not go to Japan. Finally, arrangements were made for the men to be sent home.

One of these sailors was named Hikozo Hamada (hee-koh-zoh hah-mah-dah). Mr. Hamada was encouraged by an American man to stay in the United States, learn English, and help the governments of Japan and the United States to become friendlier. Mr. Hamada was even taken to meet Pres-

ident Lincoln. After that he changed his name to Joseph Heco, because it sounded pleasant and more American to him. Joseph Heco became the first person born in Japan to become an American citizen.

Before the mid-1800s, by Japanese law people from other countries were not allowed to go to Japan, and the Japanese people could not leave. The Japanese did not want outsiders' ideas in their country. So Mr. Nakahama and Mr. Heco were very unusual. This law was challenged by an American naval officer, Matthew C. Perry, who wanted to trade with the Japanese. In 1853, Admiral Perry led some warships into Edo (eh-doh) Bay, now known as Tokyo (toh-kyoh) Bay. He demanded that Japan allow foreigners to come into the country. The Japanese government finally agreed to let people visit Japan. In 1854, the United States and Japan signed a formal treaty that opened more ports for trade.

In 1869, the Japanese government allowed the first group of Japanese to leave for the United States. These people established the Wakamatsu (wah-kah-maht-soo) Colony at Gold Hill in California. Although their colony failed, many other Japanese pioneers would follow in about ten years.

IMMIGRATION IN THE LATE 1800s

After Japan agreed to trade with the United States, many Japanese men decided to cross the Pacific Ocean in the late 1800s for education, work, and adventure. Many of the earliest travelers were students sent by the Japanese government to get an education in the West. These students were supposed to return to Japan to help the Japanese understand American ways. Others just wanted a better education in the United States.

There were other reasons Japanese men left Japan. In Japan, a family's oldest son inherited all the family property. Many men who were not first-born moved to America to get land of their own. Also, taxes in Japan were so high that some men had to leave or sell their land. A few men left because they had broken the law and didn't want to get caught or punished. Another reason for leaving was that all men between the ages of 20 and 32 had to join the army. Some men left the country rather than serve in the army for so long. Stories in the newspapers told about the success of Japanese immigrants in the United States. Others dreamed that they could find success, too.

At first, most of the Japanese men who moved to America planned to make some money, then go back to Japan to buy land, build a house, and have a family. But it

The Wing Luke Asian Museum

A group of Japanese Americans

was hard for them to save money because many prejudiced American store owners charged the Japanese higher prices. Because land prices in Japan kept rising and many immigrants had low-paying jobs in America, many men never saved up enough money to go back to Japan. Instead, they stayed in the United States.

Labor contractors (men who hired people to work in the United States) tried to convince the Japanese to come to America by offering them passage, food, and clothing. They were told that jobs would be waiting for them once they got to America, but these jobs ended up being hard ones that no one else would do. The Japanese men who came to the United States had to have strength, hope, and the courage to leave the known and travel into the unknown.

Some of the early immigrants went to the far Western United States—Hawaii, California, Oregon, Washington, or Alaska. There, labor contractors assigned them different jobs. The Japanese men weren't paid very much, but they worked really hard just the same.

Many Japanese men worked on farms as laborers. They were paid by the hour or by the day. They worked in fields on the Pacific Coast, mainly in California, and also in the Rocky Mountain states.

If farm laborers could save enough money, they could become sharecroppers. A sharecropper works on someone else's field and gets part of the money from the crops, not just an hourly wage. After saving even more money, a Japanese man could then rent land from an American. This way he could grow his own crops and keep all the money, not just a part. Once he saved enough money, he could buy his very own farm.

Japanese immigrants were very successful in farming because they knew how to take junky old land that no one wanted and turn it into a beautiful farm. They could do this because every member of the Japanese family worked hard to change the land. They drained swamplands, leveled hillsides, and cleared away forest and brush to make farm land.

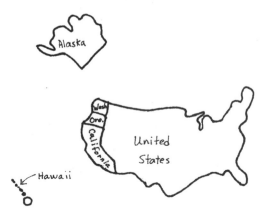

Some white wholesalers were prejudiced against the Japanese and refused to buy from Japanese American farmers. (A wholesaler is a person who buys fruits and vegetables from farmers and then sells them to the stores.) For this reason, many Japanese immigrants opened up their own businesses and sold their fruits and vegetables themselves. They sold their produce to other Japanese or to neighbors. By 1940, half of the produce on the West Coast was sold by Japanese wholesalers.

Another way the Japanese made a living was by fishing. Since Japan is an island nation, many Japanese immigrants knew how to fish when they came to America. In 1901, one dozen Japanese fishermen came to Terminal Island near Los Angeles, California. These fishermen caught fish and abalone (a kind of shellfish) in the ocean between Central America and Hawaii. By 1910, Terminal Island had three canneries where 3,000 people worked. Nearly 2,000 of these workers were Japanese. Other fishermen fished off the coast of California, Oregon, Washington, and Alaska.

Many Japanese immigrants found jobs in which they didn't need to speak a lot of English. Some men mined for gold and silver in Utah or for coal in Colorado. They also worked in lumber mills and logging camps in Oregon. Strong Japanese men helped build the railroad tracks in the mountain states (like Colorado and Idaho) and throughout the West.

Most Japanese immigrants lived in the country on farms, but some lived in the cities. Some worked in houses as cooks, servants, and gardeners. Many people hired Japanese because they were thought to be quiet, honest, and obedient.

Many Americans didn't like the Japanese, and they kept away from them. The Japanese looked and talked differently, and they ate different foods. These Americans felt that their race was better than the Japanese race. Many Americans did not trust people from other countries.

Most store owners didn't want the Japanese to shop in their stores, so the Japanese had to open their own businesses to serve their own community. They started restaurants and cafés where they cooked Japanese foods. They opened hotels, grocery stores, laundries, and barber shops. They built thriving business centers for their communities.

JAPANESE WOMEN COME TO AMERICA

Imagine you are a young woman, and your father has given you a picture of a man in his

Carolyn Takeshita

A picture bride's husband

Carolyn Takeshita

A picture bride from Japan

twenties. You don't recognize him. Who is he? You finally figure out that it is a picture of a man who wants to marry you!

Today, most people get married because they love each other. But in the old days, many marriages were arranged. That's how it was for many early Japanese immigrants. At the beginning of this century, American laws did not allow Japanese to marry other Americans who weren't Japanese. At this time there were very few Japanese women living in America. The Japanese men who immigrated to the United States had to come up with a plan to find wives. Between 1900 and 1920 pictures were exchanged, and marriages were arranged between families in Japan. The women from these marriages were often called "picture brides."

Sometimes older Japanese men in America would send pictures of themselves at a younger age, or even pictures of a different person. This was because they feared that a young woman would want to marry someone her own age. These older men were lonely. Some of them had been looking for wives for twenty years. Can you imagine how it would feel to be alone for that long when you come from a culture that really values having a family?

After exchanging pictures, the man would pay for the woman to come to the United States. Before she left Japan, the woman would get married in a traditional Japanese wedding ceremony without the groom being there. Sometimes, the woman would have to live with the husband's family after the wedding until she left for America. Once in the United States, the bride and groom got married again, this time the American way.

You might be wondering why a woman would choose to be a picture bride. She might have had hopes of becoming rich, or might just have been curious about the wonderful country called America. Some older women were afraid of never getting married or having children. Most women were not able to support themselves, because it was against Japanese custom for women to have paying jobs. Others married because it was their parents' wish. In Japan, especially in those days, you always did what your parents told you to do, no matter how old you were.

The journey to America was very difficult, with crowded quarters on steamships. Many of the travelers suffered from sea-

sickness and boredom. When the women saw their husbands for the first time, some of them broke down and cried. Some of the brides had dreamed about a rich, handsome man, only to find out that their grooms were much older, and not rich at all.

The women had to work in the fields, do housework, grow a garden, and raise animals, all while taking care of a family. They usually could not afford child care, so mothers had to take their babies to the fields. The babies sometimes died of heat, disease, drowning, or other accidents. If there was an older daughter in the family, she did all of the housework and took care of the children. Sometimes the husbands were mean, so the friendships women had with each other at work were very important to them.

Even if a woman's life was awful in America, she could not return to Japan. Her parents would be ashamed, because people would think their daughter had failed to make a life for herself in America. Many marriages succeeded only because of duty, respect, and honor.

About 20,000 Japanese women came to America between 1900 and 1920, but only some of them were picture brides. On February 28, 1920, under pressure from the United States, the Japanese government said that it would not let any more picture brides come to America. This was called the "Ladies Agreement." Many men who did not have wives yet were afraid that they would never get married. For the next three or four years, single men had to return to Japan to find their brides themselves.

GENERATIONS

In order to understand the history of Japanese Americans, it is important to know how each generation is named. The Japanese are the only Asian Americans who do this. The Japanese word *sei* (pronounced "say") means "generation or an age." *Is* (ees) comes from the word that means "one," so *Issei* means "first generation." *Ni* (nee) means "two," so *Nisei* means "second generation." And *san* (sahn) means "three," so *Sansei* means "third generation." The list below tells you the words for the first through the tenth generations:

Issei (ees-say) – first generation
Nisei (nee-say) – second generation
Sansei (sahn-say) – third generation
Yonsei (yohn-say) – fourth generation
Gosei (goh-say) – fifth generation
Rokusei (roh-koo-say) – sixth generation
Nansei (nahn-say) – seventh generation
Hachisei (hah-chee-say) – eighth generation (also *Hassei*, hah-say)
Kyusei (kyoo-say) – ninth generation
Jusei (joo-say) – tenth generation

Try to figure out which generation you belong to.

The Issei (ees-say) are people who were born in Japan and came to the United States. Most of them came between 1890 and 1924. They were not American citizens by birth, and they were not allowed to apply for citizenship until after World War II. Most of them were men. Most spoke Japanese, but some learned to speak a little English.

The Japanese were among the best-educated immigrants to the United States. Some of them had an eighth-grade education, which used to be a lot of schooling. Others even had college degrees.

The Issei felt that their values and their roots were very important. They valued education and encouraged their children to study hard. When they were sad, they found strength in the traditions they had followed in Japan. They loved each other, and their families were very special to them. They taught their children to respect nature, religion, traditional values, and their elders (an elder is anyone older than you are).

A produce store in a Japanese American community

The Issei also valued conformity, which means that they tried not to be different from anyone else in how they looked, talked, or acted. "Saving face" was also very important to them. This means that they avoided doing anything that would cause embarrassment to themselves or to their families. In Japan, farmers, workers, and craftsmen were taught to accept things that happened to them. They were taught to keep quiet and not to complain.

Many Issei helped other newcomers settle into Japanese American communities. They explained American laws and ways, and they helped new people find houses and feel welcome. They also had a saying, *"kodomo no tane ni"* (koh-doh-moh noh tah-neh nee), which means "for the sake of the children." They put up with all the mean things that people said or did to them so that their children could have a good future in America.

The *Nisei* (nee-say), or second generation, were the children of the Issei. Nisei were born in America, which made them American citizens. This made them very different from their Japan-born parents, who could not become naturalized citizens until 1952.

Nisei were raised in two cultures. They often spoke Japanese at home and English at school. They practiced American ways with their friends and some Japanese customs with their families. Nisei shared many of the same values as their parents. They went to school in America with the encouragement of their Issei parents. They also wanted to fit in with American culture. This meant they had to give up some of their Japanese customs and ways. Most of the Nisei were born between 1900 and 1940.

The *Sansei* (sahn-say) are the third generation. Like their Nisei parents, these Japanese Americans were born in America. They are American citizens, too. Some Issei feel that the Sansei have lost their Japanese traditions, language, and values, because the Sansei dress, talk, act, and think like "Americans." The Sansei generation is known for saying what is on their minds and for being more will-

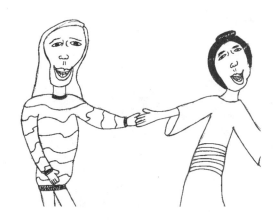

ing to stand up for themselves. Most Sansei were born between the mid-1940s and mid-1960s.

The *Yonsei* (yohn-say), or fourth generation, were born into families that had been in the U.S. for fifty years or more. They understand and take part in nearly all American events and customs. Sometimes they practice Japanese culture on special occasions. Most Yonsei have never been to Japan. Most of the authors of this book are Yonsei.

BUILDING A SENSE OF COMMUNITY

As Japanese immigrants began to settle in America, they formed organizations to help each other. One important group was the *kenjinkai* (kehn-jeen-kye). A *ken* (kehn) is a Japanese prefecture, which is like a state. People who lived in different kens had their own ways of speaking, different habits and customs, and even different churches. A kenjinkai helped people from the same prefecture solve problems and meet other people.

Courtesy of Archie A. Miyatake

The Koyasan Buddhist Temple

Contractors would often assign new laborers to work with people from the same ken. Being in a kenjinkai with people from the same ken, the laborers could continue to speak their regional dialect of Japanese, eat the food they had eaten in Japan, and even carry on trades from their area of Japan.

Religion played a very important part in the lives of many Japanese, and it still does today. All Japanese don't believe in just one religion, but often combine parts of Buddhism, Shintoism, and Christianity.

In America, many Japanese Americans practiced Buddhism or Christianity. Sometimes, these two religions worked together in the Japanese American community. The temples and churches had special ceremonies for marriage, birth, and death. They helped the Japanese immigrants learn to speak English and adopt American ways. They also taught children to be polite with their elders, friends, and strangers. They counseled women about fashion and cooking, and also helped many Japanese Amer-

icans find jobs. Some preschoolers and kindergartners took classes in temples and churches as well.

Within the Japanese American community there were clubs that people could belong to. There were several reasons for these clubs. First, the immigrants wanted to learn about their new home and new culture. Second, young men and women wanted a place to meet and get to know one another. This was good for parents, too, because they often wanted their children to marry "their own kind." A third reason was that Japanese Americans were excluded from (not allowed to join) white clubs and sports until after World War II.

The Japanese Americans formed their own athletic leagues because they were not allowed to play in other American leagues. Teams were formed based on where players lived and on how old they were. Their experiences in these leagues taught them a lot more than just how to play a game. It taught young players how to be leaders, how to talk well, and how to be on their own.

In the early 1900s, the Issei began to play baseball. It was their main enjoyment after long hours of hard work. Japanese Ameri-

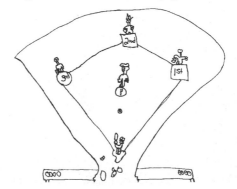

cans had baseball teams in many states. As the Nisei became older, they formed baseball teams, too, and played every Sunday. These teams had play-offs and even played for the league championship at a state level. Baseball gave them a chance to make new friends and be part of a Japanese American community.

The Nisei also formed all-Japanese basketball leagues in the late 1930s. They even had Japanese announcers. The Nisei basketball leagues became so popular that they also held statewide and national play-offs.

Other community organizations were often all Japanese American. These included the Boy and Girl Scouts, the YMCAs and YWCAs, the Campfire Girls, gardening associations, bowling leagues, *judo* (joo-doh), which is a martial art, and *kendo* (kehn-doh), which is Japanese fencing. For example, a local YMCA would sponsor a group just for Japanese Americans. These organizations gave Japanese Americans a chance to get together and visit with one another.

Leadership had a different style in the Japanese American community. A good leader in the Japanese culture was someone who knew what was going on in his community, who could work with all the different clubs and organizations, and who did not grab "the spotlight."

DISCRIMINATION AND EXCLUSION

Throughout American history, laws have been passed against non-whites. As far back as 1790, Congress passed a law stating that

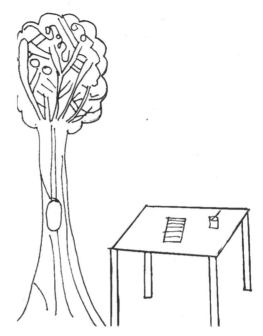

only "free white people" could become citizens of the United States. Then in 1870, Congress changed that law so that people of African ancestry could become citizens, but other non-white immigrants could not.

In 1882, the Chinese Exclusion Act was passed. This stopped Chinese people from legally entering the United States and from becoming American citizens. People who were prejudiced against the Chinese soon became angry when Japanese immigrants came to the United States to do the hard jobs once done by the Chinese.

Groups that were prejudiced against the Japanese began forming in the early 1900s. The success of the Issei made these groups angry, because they felt the immigrants were taking their jobs. They robbed and attacked many Japanese businesses. Many of these groups influenced lawmakers and

government officials. Many politicians gave speeches and tried to pass laws against Japanese immigrants. One man supporting the anti-Japanese groups was James D. Phelan, the mayor of San Francisco, California. He once said about Japanese immigrants, ". . . they are not the stuff of which American citizens are made. . . ."

By 1905, Russia and Japan had just finished a war. Japan won and Russia had to sign a treaty, and bad feelings against the Japanese started to swell in America. The war had given those who hated the Japanese an excuse to think that Japan might try to attack the United States next. They also felt the Japanese immigrants couldn't be "good Americans." For example, the lawmakers of California tried to pass laws against the Japanese people each time the legislature met from 1908 until a few years after World War II.

Another example of prejudice against the Japanese came after the big earthquake of 1906 in San Francisco. The earthquake damaged several schools and gave the San Francisco School Board an excuse to throw 93 Japanese children out of school. They were told to go to the "Oriental School" in Chinatown. The school board was trying to

establish a separate school system for the Japanese. Twenty-five of those children were American citizens of Japanese descent.

The Japanese Association protested because Chinatown was far from many Japanese immigrants' homes. The students and their families were insulted by the school board's action because they valued education and didn't want to be treated differently. Even the Japanese government protested, and President Theodore Roosevelt described the school board's action as a "wicked absurdity." In late 1907, the president convinced the school board that they should let the Japanese students back into the regular public school system.

In 1908 President Roosevelt signed the "Gentlemen's Agreement" with Japan, which said if the Japanese would stop sending workers from Japan, the United States would treat the Japanese in America more fairly. Farm labor groups in California didn't want any more workers from Japan because they felt the Japanese were taking their jobs.

At this time, women and children could still come to America, because the Gentlemen's Agreement allowed Japanese to join family members in the United States. But labor groups soon claimed that Japanese women were taking too many of the jobs and having too many children. Many people didn't like this, because the children born in the United States were American citizens, entitled to many of the same rights as other Americans. On March 1, 1920, under a lot of pressure from the United States, the Japanese government stopped giving passports to women, too.

In 1913, the Japanese American people in California had to face the Alien Land Law. This law said that since the Issei could not be legal citizens, they didn't have the right to own land in California. So, many Issei bought land in their American-born children's names. Japanese Americans could still lease land, but only for three years. Two other states, Washington and Oregon, also passed similar land laws.

In 1920, California passed the Amended Alien Land Law. The new law didn't allow any Issei to buy or rent land either for themselves or under the names of their children who were American citizens.

In 1922, Congress passed the Cable Act, which said that any American woman who married a new immigrant could lose her own citizenship. If the marriage ended because of death or divorce, a white woman of European descent could regain her American citizenship, but a Japanese American woman who was a citizen could not.

Two years later, Congress passed the Immigration Act of 1924. This act said that no more Asian immigrants could come to America. It stopped any more Japanese from legally coming to the United States. People in Japan got very angry, and Japan's relationship with the United States started to head in the wrong direction. Japanese Americans also got angry because their Fourteenth Amendment rights were being ignored. This amendment states that no law can be passed that discriminates against a person on the basis of race, color, or creed. The Immigration Act didn't change until 1952.

WORLD WAR II (1939–1945)

In 1931, Japan was preparing to take over Asia. The Japanese people needed more living space, food, and raw materials such as oil, metal, and rubber. President Franklin D. Roosevelt wanted to stop Japan. By 1937, Japan and the United States had broken off business relations. In 1939, President Roosevelt ordered Navy ships to be stationed at Pearl Harbor in Hawaii as a warning to Japan. (Hawaii is 6,000 miles east of Japan across the Pacific, 3,000 miles closer to Japan than the West Coast is.) The commander of the Japanese Navy thought that a surprise attack would greatly hurt the U.S. Navy and that Japan would then be free to take over Asia.

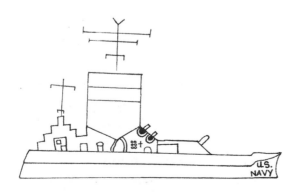

On December 7, 1941, the Japanese Imperial Forces bombed Pearl Harbor. The fears many Americans felt about anyone of Japanese descent grew stronger. Now, many Americans had no trust at all in the Japanese. On December 8, the U.S. Congress declared war on Japan. Within hours, the FBI arrested 736 Japanese people in Hawaii and on the U.S. mainland, because they feared these people might be spies and help the enemy. By mid-February, just two months after the bombing of Pearl Harbor, more than 2,000 Japanese Americans had been put in jail by the government. These were Issei and Nisei community leaders, including teachers, priests, and newspaper editors.

The war continued to get bigger and more dangerous as the Axis Powers (Germany, Italy, and Japan) fought against the Allies (Great Britain, the Soviet Union, the United States, and 73 other nations). Prejudice against the Japanese grew. On January 5, 1942, about a month after the U.S. entered the war, the War Department said Japanese American men could not volunteer to be in the U.S. Army. The War Department thought that Japanese American men of draft age were America's enemies. Those men who were already in the U.S. military were kicked out.

A lieutenant commander named Kenneth Duval Ringle was assigned to learn all he could about Japanese American loyalty. The report he wrote, and other secret reports written by the Navy, said that Japanese Americans were loyal citizens to the United States. The reports argued against mass

internment of Japanese Americans. (Internment means to confine people to an area or a camp, especially during wartime.) Even so, on February 19, 1942, President Franklin D. Roosevelt signed Executive Order 9066. This gave the Secretary of War the power to put any person felt to be a threat to the United States into an internment camp. In all, about 110,000 Japanese Americans were sent to internment camps during World War II.

INTERNMENT CAMPS

In American history books, several names are used to describe the places where Japanese Americans were sent during World War II. The places set up by the War Relocation Authority were called "relocation camps." The Justice Department ran "internment camps," like the one in Crystal City, Texas, that were separate from the relocation camps. The War Relocation Authority also set up camps that were called "citizen isolation centers" near Leupp, Arizona, and Moab, Utah. These

This map shows many of the places where Japanese people were held during World War II. Japanese people who lived in the area that is shaded were ordered to move to an internment camp. The names in small letters were "assembly centers." The two names with a dot next to them were "citizen isolation centers." The names in big letters were permanent internment camps.

centers were for people the government thought were troublemakers. Other people called these centers "detention camps." As early as October 20, 1942, President Roosevelt and other high-ranking government officials called the places "concentration camps." Some people call all of these places "concentration camps."

The authors of this book decided not to use the term "concentration camps." This is out of respect for the millions of Jewish people and others who were killed in Nazi concentration camps in Germany during World War II. Most Japanese Americans feel that the names "relocation camps" and "detention camps" do not really describe the hardship, shame, and loss of freedom

they experienced. For these reasons, we will use the name "internment camps" in this book.

When Executive Order 9066 went into effect, people of Japanese descent on the West Coast were first put under a curfew and then ordered to "evacuate" within 48 hours. The curfew was a law that said that Japanese Americans couldn't be on the street after a certain time. The police put anyone who looked Japanese in jail if they broke the curfew, even if they were loyal American citizens.

The order to "evacuate" meant that Japanese Americans had to leave their homes and go to one of 16 "assembly centers" in California, Washington, or Arizona. These centers

were odd places like horse racetracks and fairgrounds, and people had to live in them for one to eight months while the interment camps were being built. While they were in the assembly centers, the Japanese Americans were not told what was going to happen to them or even where they were going.

Some people moved to other states, out of the boundaries that the government had set up, to escape being sent to a camp. Military leaders felt more threatened by Japanese Americans on the West Coast. This was because 95 percent of Japanese Americans lived on the West Coast, and, after Pearl Harbor, their large numbers frightened others. But while some Japanese Americans left the West Coast, most stayed and followed orders to evacuate. Many were afraid there would be violence if they disobeyed. Many people lost everything they owned, including their businesses, cars, houses, and possessions. They could

take only what they could carry with them to the camps.

In the last months of 1942, Japanese Americans were sent to one of ten permanent internment camps. These camps were in California, Nevada, Arizona, Utah, New Mexico, Idaho, Wyoming, Colorado, and Arkansas. Some camps, like the one in Tule Lake, California, had 18,000 people—that's as many as a medium-sized town. Some were smaller, like the one in Granada, Colorado, which had 7,000 people. One of the Justice Department internment camps was in Crystal City, Texas, where Japanese Americans and others who were thought to be spies were sent.

All of this cost the U.S. government a lot of money, and yet there was never any proof that Japanese Americans were not loyal American citizens. All the camps were located in isolated areas, away from other people. The people were always being

watched from towers by guards with guns in their hands. It was enough to scare anyone! The years spent in the camps made many Japanese Americans feel guilty for things they did not do and left them feeling frustrated.

Conditions in the internment camps were awful. People lived in long, barrack-style, tar-papered buildings surrounded by barbed wire. There were 12 to 14 barracks in a block, and a total of 250 to 300 people lived in a single block. Each barrack had about six rooms. A whole family had to live in one room, and there might be as many as eight people in a family. Sometimes small families had to share a room with another family. The rooms were small, cramped, and dirty. In some, the walls didn't go all the way up to the ceiling. Everybody could hear everything that went on in the whole building.

One of the worst things about the housing was that family members did not have privacy inside their own room. People sometimes hung blankets on a rope to make separate rooms. Even bathrooms were not private and had to be shared by everyone. People felt very uncomfortable and crowded, living with no privacy in such a large group of people. Can you imagine living under such conditions?

The people in the internment camps tried to entertain themselves by forming sewing and craft classes, and playing sports like baseball. Sometimes they drew pictures and wrote poetry and stories about life in the camps. They did this because they were

pah), which is Chinese cabbage. They did everything they could to make life as comfortable as they could.

After several months, each camp started a school for the children. All of the teachers taught American history and the Pledge of Allegiance. We think it is amazing that Japanese Americans were forced to salute the American flag and pledge their loyalty to a country whose government had put them into an internment camp. People were not allowed to speak Japanese, and all teaching was done in English.

Not many people know this, but in Hawaii there were two internment camps, called Sand Island and Honouliuli. There were more than 421,000 people of Japanese descent in Hawaii, many more than on the U.S. mainland. But the government did not order a major evacuation in Hawaii. More than 1,500 people were arrested in Hawaii, and 1,250 of them were eventually sent to one of the camps. But they were all given a hearing, which is a chance to defend yourself in court. Some people were allowed to go back to their homes. The Japanese Americans on the mainland were never given a hearing.

The reason that people living in Hawaii were treated differently from people living on the West Coast was that businesses in Hawaii depended on the Japanese Americans for labor and customers. If all people in Hawaii of Japanese descent had been put into camps, many stores would have gone out of business, and the owners of sugar cane fields would not have had enough laborers. Because the Japanese Americans in Hawaii were not all rounded up and sent

not allowed to bring their cameras to take pictures that would show what happened in the camps.

The food at the camps was not the greatest—in fact, it was terrible! The same thing was often served day after day. At Poston, an internment camp in Arizona, a meal was once potato hash and moldy bread.

The weather was a big concern, too. Since the barracks were poorly built, the cracks let in the dirt and rain. Can you imagine sweeping your room every time the wind blew? At many of the camps the summer brought temperatures of more than 100 degrees in the shade, and the winters were freezing cold.

The adults did many things to make their new homes better. They built sports fields and schools. They raised chickens and grew vegetables like sugar beets and nappa (nah-

World Times News

Most Decorated Team

442nd Combat Team of all Japanese Americans have won more medals and decorations than any other military unit in American history.

to internment camps, the Nisei men from Hawaii were the first Japanese Americans to volunteer to serve their country in the U.S. Army.

In September 1945, the U.S. government admitted it was against the law to hold loyal American citizens in the internment camps. The Japanese Americans in the camps were told to leave the camps and return home.

SERVING OUR COUNTRY

In 1942, all Japanese Americans in the armed services were kicked out. Some pushed for the reopening of the draft to prove their loyalty to America, while other Japanese Americans didn't want to fight until they had their rights restored. The government realized that having interpreters who could speak Japanese was important, so the ban was lifted in 1943.

While many Japanese Americans spent World War II in internment camps, others left the camps to risk their lives fighting for their country. During the war, Japanese Americans served in the 442nd Regimental Combat Team, the Military Intelligence Service, the 100th Battalion, the 552nd

Field Artillery Battalion, and the Women's Army Corps. Many women also served in the army as nurses or translators. By the end of World War II, more than 33,000 Nisei had served in the armed forces.

On February 1, 1943, the 442nd Regimental Combat Team was created. About 4,500 Japanese American men came from the mainland and Hawaii to join. They trained for the Army at Camp Shelby in Mississippi. These soldiers fought many battles during World War II. The most famous ones were in France, one in the town of Bruyeres and one called the Battle of the Lost Battalion, where they rescued soldiers from Texas. About 1,000 Japanese American soldiers died to rescue 250 men.

The 442nd Regimental Combat Team became famous because they were all Japanese Americans, and they won more medals and decorations than any other military unit in American history. They fought for their country even though their moms, dads, wives, and children were behind barbed wire in the internment camps. One man, named Sadao Munemori (sah-dah-oh moo-neh-mohree), won a medal because he threw himself on a hand grenade to save two of the men in his platoon.

Many people don't know this, but the men in the 552nd Field Artillery were among the first Allied troops to rescue prisoners from Dachau, a German concentration camp. Many of the prisoners in the camp were sick, starving, or dying. The Japanese American soldiers were told not to give the prisoners food, clothes, or med-

ical help, but they did anyway. They were told not to talk about the rescue, so they never got credit for being at Dachau. Most history books do not mention their actions, either.

The U.S. government asked other Japanese Americans who could speak, read, and write Japanese to fight for America by being interpreters. These Japanese Americans were in the Military Intelligence Service (MIS). Many of the men and women in the MIS had to work for America while their families were in the internment camps, too. The work they did was really secret, and for many years no one knew about them or about what kind of work they did to help in World War II.

The war ended when President Harry Truman ordered the military to bomb the Japanese cities of Nagasaki (nah-gah-sah-kee) and Hiroshima (hee-roh-shee-mah) in August 1945. This was the first time in history that atomic bombs were used,

and it changed the world forever. Many Japanese Americans were glad the war was finally over, but they were also very sad because they had relatives who were hurt or killed in the bombings. Some Japanese Americans in the MIS were sent to Nagasaki and Hiroshima to translate for the people who survived the bombings.

CHALLENGING THE U.S. GOVERNMENT

When Japanese Americans were put under a curfew in 1942, some people protested. Many people said that the curfew was unconstitutional, that it took away rights guaranteed by the U.S. Constitution.

Four people who were put in jail for breaking curfew were Gordon Hirabayashi (hee-rah-bah-yah-shee), Minoru Yasui (mee-noh-roo yah-soo-ee), Fred Korematsu (koh-reh-mah-tsoo), and Mitsuye Endo (meet-soo-eh ehn-doh). They went to court to fight for their rights, but they lost their cases. Many years after the war these people went to court again because they felt they had been unjustly convicted. They had been put in camps, but they hadn't done anything wrong. Mitsuye Endo's case was decided in 1944. Although the court decided that she was a loyal citizen and let her out of the camp, they didn't discuss what had happened.

Another group of people who challenged the U.S. government were some Nisei men from the Heart Mountain camp near Cody, Wyoming. They did not want to be drafted

Courtesy of Archie A. Miyatake

A large group of Japanese people becoming American citizens

into the army until their constitutional rights were given back to them. They said they would agree to be drafted if their families were let out of the camps. The government said no to this. Some of the men who didn't want to be drafted had to go to prison for three years because they stood up for their rights.

AFTER WORLD WAR II

Over time, the government and the American people began to see that the Japanese Americans had been unfairly treated during World War II. In 1948, President Truman signed the Japanese American Evacuation Claims Act, which promised to pay Japanese Americans back for what they had lost when they were sent to the camps. But the act said that they needed to show exact records proving what they had lost. Most did not have any records, and besides, the hard work they had put into building a farm or a business could never be paid back with money. Other Japanese Americans felt that the government should repay them not only with money but with an apology, too.

After they were told to leave the camps, the Japanese Americans had a hard time starting over because they had lost so much money, property, and time. The average age of an Issei woman after the war was 47. The average age of an Issei man was 55, and the average age of Nisei children was 17. It was almost impossible to make enough money to buy what they needed to start all over. But most Japanese Americans believed in hard work, honesty, not giving up, independence, and doing high-quality work. These beliefs helped them to go back to their communities to build their lives again.

After World War II, many Japanese Americans and Issei went to court to make Congress understand that treating them like foreigners, and sometimes even enemies, was not constitutional. Congress was convinced and, in 1952, passed an act called the McCarran-Walter Immigration and Naturalization Act. This act allowed Japanese Issei to become American citizens for the first time. Soon after this act was passed, thousands of Issei became citizens of the United States.

Even though many Japanese Americans had college educations, they still had a hard time getting jobs and buying homes, because some Americans were still prejudiced. The only businesses Issei were allowed to work in were farming, fishing, and small businesses inside the Japanese American community. Yet, by the late 1960s, because of their hard work, many Nisei and Sansei were just as well off as white Americans of European descent.

The Japanese American struggle was really hard on the Issei. They were having a hard time living the way they had lived before World War II and the internment camps. Some of the Nisei spoke out about their hard times, but most were quiet and did not want to talk about their life in the camps. The Sansei got the Nisei to talk about the camps and their experiences. Many of the Sansei wanted Japanese Americans to tell their story to the public and to fight for their constitutional rights. The Sansei were too young to remember or to share the feelings of their Nisei parents or Issei grandparents, so they helped their elders speak out. The Sansei felt that most Americans believed Japanese Americans to be quiet and obedient (always obeying), and they wanted to change this stereotype.

The Wing Luke Asian Museum

A Japanese American family in front of their restaurant

THE WHITE HOUSE
WASHINGTON

A monetary sum and words alone cannot restore lost years or erase painful memories; neither can they fully convey our Nation's resolve to rectify injustice and to uphold the rights of individuals. We can never fully right the wrongs of the past. But we can take a clear stand for justice and recognize that serious injustices were done to Japanese Americans during World War II.

In enacting a law calling for restitution and offering a sincere apology, your fellow Americans have, in a very real sense, renewed their traditional commitment to the ideals of freedom, equality, and justice. You and your family have our best wishes for the future.

Sincerely,

GEORGE BUSH
PRESIDENT OF THE UNITED STATES

OCTOBER 1990

A letter from President George Bush apologizing for the U.S. government's treatment of Japanese Americans during World War II

Many Sansei never learned to speak, read, or write Japanese, because they were not allowed to speak the language in the internment camps. It is sad that they lost this part of their heritage, and it made many Issei feel cut off from their grandchildren. Some Sansei are now starting to learn the language of their heritage.

REDRESS

In the 1960s, many minorities, including Japanese Americans, began looking back into their histories. They wanted to learn more about themselves, to find out who they were and where their beliefs came from. Martin Luther King, who led the civil rights movement for African Americans, and Cesar Chavez, who led the migrant farm workers in California, were two men who inspired Japanese Americans to fight for their own rights.

Japanese Americans studied the history of World War II and realized how unfairly their people had been treated. In the 1970s, many Japanese Americans felt that they should do something about it. They wanted the U.S. government to apologize to the Japanese Americans for what had happened

during the war, and to recognize that they took away the Japanese Americans' constitutional rights. They called this action "redress," which means "to correct" or "to repay." It wasn't really the money that the Sansei wanted. They wanted an apology. Another goal of redress was to teach people about what had happened to Japanese Americans so that it would never happen again to any group of people.

In 1980, President Jimmy Carter ordered a group of officials to study the internment camps and Executive Order 9066. This group decided that the Japanese Americans had been treated unfairly and should get both an apology and money.

Many Japanese American organizations got together to work on getting a bill passed in Congress. Other people besides Japanese Americans also helped. The cases of Hirabayashi, Yasui, and Korematsu were also being re-tried around the same time, so a lot of attention was put on this bill. The bill was called the Civil Liberties Act of 1988, and it was signed by President Ronald Reagan. By passing this act, the U.S. government admitted that it had made a mistake in putting Japanese Americans into internment camps, and it paid them a sum of money. The first letter of apology was signed by President George Bush in 1990. As you can see, it took a long time to get an apology.

Some Japanese Americans were happy when they received their letter of apology and the money. Others didn't want anything. They just wanted to forget their experiences in the camps. For others, the money was a help, although it could never repay them for their years in the camps, and the apology helped them to believe again in the U.S. Constitution. Today, many people spend time teaching other Americans about what really happened to Japanese Americans during World War II.

CONCLUSION

Even though the Japanese Americans got money and an apology for what was done to them during World War II, they still face some racism and prejudice. We hope this book helps people understand what happened to the Japanese Americans, so that no one is treated unfairly because of where they came from, how they look, what language they speak, or what they believe.

We have learned that the Issei tried to make a good life in America. They put up with a lot of hardship so that their children would have a better life. This is why most immigrants come to the United States. The Nisei tried to fit into their new culture and home, but they tried to keep their traditional Japanese ways alive, too. Many Nisei were not told about their parents' experiences. Today, the Sansei and Yonsei, the third and fourth generations, have had time to think about these events. They want to learn as much as possible about their heritage, culture, and history. They also want to share what they know, because Japanese American history is a part of American history.

OUR FAMILIES' STORIES

It's fun to look back through your family tree,
And learn about your grandparents' history.
Picture brides, internment camps, and stories galore.
Things from the past, to learn and explore.

Here we share the stories of our grandparents. Each one is very special to us. These stories will help you understand the lives of people who came before us.

Grandpa's Letter
by Zeni Whittall

When I was in the sixth grade, my class studied World War II. There was no reference to the Japanese American internment camps in our history books. I wanted people to know what had happened to thousands of Japanese Americans, less than fifty years ago, because I am half Japanese American. I wrote a letter to my grandfather and asked him if he would tell me about what happened.

This letter is the only time that my grandfather shared his story with anyone in my

Zeni Whitfall with his grandfather

family in writing. My grandfather was Nisei Japanese American. Many times before, my mother had asked him what had happened in the camp, but because of the pain and the shame, he could not share it with her. Many other Japanese Americans who were interned have not shared their painful memories with their children either. After reparations from the government, however, they are now finding the strength to tell their grandchildren.

I am sharing this letter with you because I want this to be remembered. My grandfather can never tell his story again because he has passed away. So read this and remember what has happened, and never let it happen again.

Dear Zeni,
I'll be glad to give you a brief outline of my experience during our relocation from the West Coast by the U.S. government.

As I recall, we were living on a small truck farm in Dominguez, California. About March or April of 1942, my dad, mother, little sister, and I were told to pack everything that we could into my dad's car, and go to San Pedro. From there we drove "caravan style" with military escorts to Santa Anita race track in Arcadia. This was called Santa Anita Assembly Center.

Once there, my dad's car was taken and sold. We were directed to the stable area where we filled bags with straw for mattresses. The stable area became our home for the next six months. We ate in army style "mess halls" and took community showers. Since I was ten years old, I had

to go to school, which was set up in the grandstands. The adults, though, were put to work making camouflage nets.

About September 1942, we were moved to Jerome, Arkansas, by train. The total trip took over a week, and the whole way we were guarded by military police. The drapes on the train were drawn the whole trip, and we were forbidden to look out. The camp was in a remote area away from anything. There were guard towers and the whole camp was fenced with barbed wire. I remember all the different wildlife; poisonous snakes, fireflies, and flying squirrels. The weather was hot and humid in the summer, but in the winter it was cold and even snowed on occasion.

While in the camp I got to join the Boy Scouts, and my troop was able to go out to be with other troops during jamborees. During all of this, I was too young to really know what was going on, so I just had fun. I would play games with the other kids in camp and we had the great outdoors. I guess it was just like a very long summer.

Around July or August of 1944, we

moved to another camp in Gila River, Arizona. What a contrast to Arkansas—first a hot, humid climate and then a desert. While here, my dad left camp to go to work in Idaho. Later he was preparing to send for us, but my mom wanted to be anything but a part of Idaho. Since the order that banned us from the West Coast was lifted, my mom made arrangements for us to return to California.

About September 1945, we were back in Los Angeles. We were very fortunate because the people my father leased his farm from before the war were very kind. They helped my dad get back on his feet by giving us some furnishings.

You asked me how I felt about what happened then and now. As I said before, I was pretty young when all of this happened. I didn't know what it was all about, except the fact that America and Japan were at war. I met a lot of people, shared many experiences, and overall I don't think that it scared me all that much. Today I feel very sad for all of the older people like my dad and also the college students. They knew it was wrong and they fought for over forty years to get the U.S. government to acknowledge the mistake that had been imposed on thousands, the forceful relocation of the Japanese Americans from the coast.

In October of 1988 President Ronald Reagan signed the Civil Liberties Act of 1988, which was the formal apology to all of the Japanese Americans who had been interned during World War II.

Love, Grandpa

Chris Tucker

A monument honoring Governor Ralph Carr in Sakura Square in Denver

My Grandpa's Story
by Harold Sampson, Jr.

After Franklin Roosevelt signed Executive Order 9066, some of my relatives had to leave California or be put in internment camps. However, grandfather's family had a choice. They could go to an internment camp or move to Colorado where they would be free. They decided to move out.

They traveled by caravan (one car, two pickups, and one truck) through Arizona and New Mexico. As they drove through towns and cities, people threw trash and garbage at them. They were not allowed to stop to rest. They were escorted by the state police through the states of Arizona and New Mexico, and were only allowed to buy gas for the car and hamburgers to eat.

When they got to the border of Colorado, a state patrolman met them and said, "Welcome to Colorado. Governor Ralph Carr and the people of Colorado welcome you. Is there anything I can help you with?" Governor Carr had sent this patrolman to meet the caravan and offer them help. He was a great man and the only governor to welcome the Japanese Americans to his state. This is why the Japanese American community in Denver built a special monument for Governor Carr in the beautiful garden at Sakura Square in Denver.

Grandpa Ozaki's Story
by Meg Ozaki

This is a story of my grandpa, Motoichi Ozaki (moh-toh-ee-chee oh-zah-kee), or Joe M. Ozaki, who was born and lived in Shingu (sheen-goo), Wakayama Ken (wah-kah-yah-mah kehn) Japan. At the age of twenty, Grandpa moved to Peru with his cousin for a better job. They lived with their aunt and uncle for a year. Grandpa got a job selling cloth, stockings, and underwear. Working at the store was an exciting experience. Once he had to stay up all night and guard it with a gun to protect it from looters. He worked there for three years and then quit. When Grandpa's aunt and uncle went back to Japan, he took over their flooring business.

Meg Ozaki with her grandfather, Motoichi "Joe" Ozaki

On August 13, 1940, Tamiye Saki (tah-mee-yeh sah-kee), his arranged wife, came from Japan to marry him. They celebrated with a few close friends. Their first child was born on May 21, 1942. They named him Francisco Kuniaki (koo-nee-ah-kee) Ozaki. He is my father.

Grandpa recalls the day he learned of the bombing of Pearl Harbor. He and grandma were driving to Lima from the beach, listening to the car radio when a news flash interrupted the music and told of the attack. From then on things started changing slowly. First, detectives started making lists of Japanese business workers in Lima. Then the government passed a law forbidding any Japanese to go more than five miles away from the city. After that, Grandpa's business slowed down and he started losing employees. Finally, in February of 1943, Peruvian detectives took him from Lima to a government detention center.

The next morning Grandpa was taken to Crystal City, an internment camp near San Antonio, Texas. Peru shipped all the Japanese in the country to internment camps in the U.S. Grandma and my father joined him six months later.

During the long years in camp, Grandpa helped write a Japanese newspaper. The people were allowed to bring only $300 apiece when they came to the camp. Grandpa's family used all their money on food.

In the camp, the family grew. Two baby girls were born and Grandpa's father, who had been living in an internment camp in Santa Fe, New Mexico, was sent to Crystal City at Grandpa's request.

Grandpa had the freedom he had in Peru taken away from him, but his philosophy was still to make the best of things.

After the war was over, his family stayed in the camp until it was ready to close. Peru had told him not to come back, because he was not a citizen. The only places in the United States that would accept the Peruvian Japanese were Seabrook Farms in New Jersey and the state of Colorado.

Grandpa found relatives in Colorado and took his family there. He has lived there since September of 1946.

My Grandma's Story
by Dara Domoto

My grandma's head throbbed with worry as she read the newspaper headlines: "U.S. Drops Atomic Bomb on Hiroshima and Nagasaki: Japan Surrenders!" Grandma Domoto (doh-moh-toh) thought immediately of her family who lived near Hiroshima. Did they get hurt? Were they alive? She had not been able to write to

Dara Domoto reading a story with Grandma Domoto

My great-grandma Kinoshita (kee-nohsh-tah), who lived in Colorado, found out that most of her family in Nagasaki were all right, except that one of her nine brothers and sisters was killed in the war. Even though she had family in Japan, Great-grandma still felt that her own sons should fight for the United States. She was proud when two of her sons joined the armed services.

Our family was lucky that many of our relatives survived a very sad time.

We learned a lot talking to our grandparents and writing a part of our family's history. You might want to do this for your family, too. It would make a neat present to give to someone you love.

them since the beginning of World War II, when she and grandpa were sent from California to an internment camp in Colorado. They lived in the camp for four years. Can you imagine how terrible it would be, not knowing about your family for that long?

After the war, my grandparents were let out of camp and went back to California, only to find all of their stored belongings gone. One good thing did happen, though. Grandma got a letter from her family telling her they were all right. Her brother told her that he biked into Hiroshima from their farm a couple days after the bombing. He was sad to see people suffering with maggots and flies in their open wounds. There wasn't enough medicine to treat everyone. It must have been a terrible sight.

Dara's great-grandma Kinoshita and her son Carl

CULTURE AND THE ARTS

Culture is fun for everyone.
The sounds of music and the beauty in art,
The festivals people celebrate,
All these customs show what's in the heart.

This chapter tells you about Japanese American cultural arts and festivals. Japanese Americans enjoy the beauty of art, the rhythm of music, and the joy of dancing, especially at celebrations and festivals, where the people come together as a community. Many Americans from other backgrounds also enjoy these parts of Japanese American culture.

We discovered that the qualities of calmness, patience, concentration, and determination are important to all of these activities. In this chapter, we feature some neat artists, some awesome "moves" in the martial arts, and recommend some cool music.

FESTIVALS

On New Year's Day carps wave from the
poles,
And rice is always in the bowls!
We liked these festivals and holidays,
We learned about them in many ways.

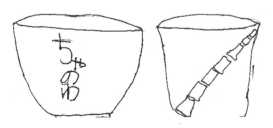

Oshogatsu

New Year's Day, or Oshogatsu (oh-shoh-gaht-soo), is celebrated on January 1 by many Japanese Americans across our nation. It is the most important, festive, and memorable occasion of the year. It is a time for special decorations, food, and traditions. The Japanese American New Year's celebration, including the decorating, cleaning, cooking, and visiting, all came from Japan. But it is slightly different in our country because it has become a mixture of Japanese tradition and American customs.

Since food is such an important part of this celebration, families prepare special foods like carp, which represents determination, and *soba* (soh-bah) noodles, which represent long life. They also cook *daikon* (dy-kohn), a Japanese radish which represents happiness; *mochi* (moh-chee), sweet rice balls that represent good fortune; *kombu* (kohm-boo), seaweed that represents happiness; *kuro mame* (koo-roh mah-meh), black beans that represent good luck; and *sake* (sah-keh), rice wine. At the end of each year, people eat a bowl of *soba*, which is buckwheat noodle soup. Soba noodles stand for money and riches, and are a lucky charm.

Mochi tsuki (moh-chee tsoo-kee), sweet rice ball making, is a special part of the New Year's celebration. Today in Japan, mochi tsuki is done by rural families and temples. Japanese American candy stores, bakeries, and families and groups get together to make and eat mochi.

Another tradition that is still followed by Japanese Americans is cleaning. House

cleaning is done until it is perfect! Cooking and house cleaning are done before the first few days of the New Year have begun. The idea is to start the new year with a clean slate. If you owe people money, you should pay it at this time. Also, personal problems should be solved. *Bonen kai* (boh-nehn kye), year-end parties, are given by companies, clubs, and friends to encourage friendships and to wish each other good luck.

On Oshogatsu, many Japanese Americans get up early and wish each family member, "Happy New Year!" In Japanese, you would say, *"Shinnen Akemashite Omedetto Gozaimasu,"* pronounced "sheen-nehn ah-keh-mahsh-teh oh-meh-deh-toh goh-zy-ee-mahs." Everyone dresses up in new clothes and visits friends and relatives. They enjoy eating *ozoni* (oh-zoh-nee), a soup with pieces of mochi (pounded rice cake), vegetables, and fish. Ozoni represents a long and good life.

Hina Matsuri

Hina Matsuri (hee-nah maht-soo-ree) means "Girls' Day." It is a day when families honor girls, in Japan and America. Hina Matsuri is on March 3 of each year. In Japan, the peach blossoms bloom in the spring. They represent happiness in marriage to women.

Families in Japan and the United States want their daughters to grow up and have happy lives. Parents in Japan want their daughters to be happy by having good marriages. They celebrate Girls' Day to teach their daughters how to be good wives who are kind, gentle, and peaceful. In America, Japanese American families want their daughters to choose their own lives, which could be a career or marriage or a combination of both.

When Japanese Americans celebrate Hina Matsuri, they follow the examples set by their grandparents and show respect for their culture by observing the day. Some Japanese Ameri-

cans display special Japanese dolls on Hina Matsuri.

Girls display the dolls that are most important to them. The very precious dolls called *Hina Ningyo* (hee-nah neen-gyoh), or "miniature dolls," represent the Imperial Court of Japan from 300 years ago. These dolls are dressed in kimonos and are surrounded by miniature horns, dressers, chairs, tables, pictures, and other tiny household things. They are displayed on a *hina-dan* (hee-nah dahn), a doll stand, which is covered with a red cloth. The hina-dan has five to seven tiers, or steps, built into it. The dolls are arranged by their place of honor, so the Emperor and Empress are on the top. The Imperial Court sets are rare and expensive, so few Japanese Americans own them.

Some people display their dolls in their home, or at a church or community center. If it is a large celebration, one or more sets of the Imperial Court dolls and other valuable Japanese dolls might be displayed in a large room. When Japanese Americans display their dolls, they want to teach others about Japanese culture, so they might also prepare Japanese food for the visitors to eat.

Tango No Sekku

May 5 is *Tango No Sekku* (tahn-goh noh seh-koo), the annual Boys' Day festival in the Japanese American community. On this day, families with one or more sons put up a bamboo flagpole

in their yards. From the poles they hang carp (fish) kites or wind socks. (We tell you how to make a wind sock in the Hands-On Fun chapter.) Carps stand for bravery, strength, and determination, qualities that families want their sons to have. The biggest carp wind sock represents the oldest son and the smallest carp represents the youngest son. The wind socks are hollow, and when the wind blows and fills the inside, the fish seem to be swimming. Some carp kites or wind socks are over eight feet long.

Inside the house, many families display warrior dolls, armor, helmets, and other things that represent strength. As you can see, strength is a very important quality for boys in Japanese American culture. These objects are very expensive and detailed, so they are displayed only on important days.

In Japan, the boys often bathe in water that has been soaked in the leaves of the iris plant. The leaves are shaped like a sword and also stand for strength. Boys also

eat a special meal of rice wrapped in the leaves of iris, bamboo, or oak for good luck and, of course, strength. This part of the custom is not usually followed here in America.

We would like you to know a little of the history to Boys' Day. According to an ancient Japanese legend, one day a boy named Kintaro (keen-tah-roh) stood beside a river, watching some fishermen. Suddenly, he saw a man-eating carp swimming toward the men. The fishermen

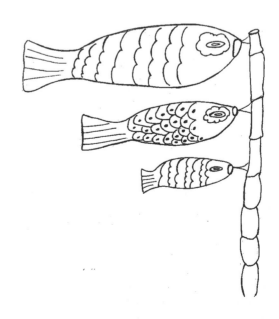

didn't notice the carp, so Kintaro jumped into the river. He fought with the fish and killed it. Ever since then, on May 5, the festival of Boys' Day has been celebrated in Japan.

In Japan, you see many colorful carp kites and wind socks flying, because Boys' Day is such a big festival. Tango No Sekku is not as big a deal in America, because it falls on the same day as El Cinco de Mayo (The Fifth of May), a day celebrated by Hispanics, so Tango No Sekku sometimes falls by the wayside. If you want to celebrate both cultures, you could fly your carp wind sock, eat somen noodles, and display your warrior dolls, as well as hit the piñata and eat tostadas.

Obon

Obon (oh-bohn), or *Bon* (bohn), is a festival for Buddhists to welcome the spirits of the dead. It's kind of like Memorial Day. Obon is also called "the Festival of Lanterns" because colorful lanterns are displayed.

Japanese Americans observe Obon between July 15 and August 15. Obon has become a part of Japanese American culture and is certainly one of the most colorful festivals of the year. For people who are Buddhist, Obon is a time to pay respect to the Buddhist way of life. They look back

upon the love, affection, compassion, and qualities that their parents and others who have died gave them while they were alive.

Japanese American Buddhists celebrate Obon with a service. Although it is a memorial service, a festive mood exists. People wear light, colorful summer cotton kimonos called *yukata* (yoo-kah-tah). The importance of Obon is to teach *kansha* (kahn-shah), which is gratitude toward parents and ancestors. It also stresses the importance of *dana* (dah-nah), or selfless giving, which should be practiced by family members, close friends, and, of course, all of us.

During this celebration, people gather in the streets and the temples to dance. *Bon-Odori* (bohn oh-doh-ree), an Obon dance, is a dance of rejoicing for the gifts of relatives who have died. These folk dances are rhythmic and simple. The young and old dance together.

Obon is celebrated in both large and small cities that have Japanese American Buddhist communities, including San Francisco, Chicago, New York, Seattle, Denver, and Honolulu. It has become a community activity where both Buddhists and Christians celebrate and remember their Japanese roots together.

Sakura Matsuri

In March or April, the Japanese people celebrate a change of the season. They go to the mountains to see the *sakura* (sah-koo-rah)—the cherry blossoms—and picnic with their friends. The short life of the sakura adds a sadness to their beauty. For this reason, the Japanese see them as more important than other flowers.

Many years ago, the Japanese government presented some cherry trees to the United States as a gift. Now, every April, many Japanese Americans and other people visit Washington, D.C., to see and participate in the Cherry Blossom Festival. Many communities in the United States have Cherry Blossom Festivals. It has become a time for Japanese Americans to gather with friends and family, and share their culture and food through demonstrations, parades, food bazaars, and carnivals.

Nisei Week

One of the largest Japanese American festivals in the United States is called Nisei Week. It is celebrated in Little Tokyo in Los Angeles, California.

The first Nisei Week was held August 12-18, 1934. That year, the Nisei (second generation) wanted the Issei (first generation) to attract business back to Little Tokyo. They wanted more people to work and do their shopping in Little Tokyo, because the Great Depression had hurt everyone's business. They decided to hold a big festival to attract business to Little Tokyo. The Nisei held a beauty contest and a baby contest, and had a parade with Japanese Amer-

Courtesy of *Tozai Times*

A Nisei Week parade in Los Angeles

ican groups like Girl and Boy Scouts, bowling and baseball teams, floats, and dancers in kimonos.

During World War II, Nisei Week was not held because so many Japanese Americans had been sent to internment camps in 1941 and 1942. Four years after the war ended, Nisei Week started again as a way to attract the Nisei and Sansei (third generation) to Little Tokyo.

Nisei Week is still celebrated today and includes Japanese American art exhibits and demonstrations, a fashion show, baby contests, martial arts contests, banquets honoring Issei pioneers, a carnival, a beauty contest, and a parade. It is such a big celebration that it is on television in Los Angeles. Some of the grand marshals of the parade have been famous people, such as the movie star Noriyuki "Pat" Morita (moh-ree-tah), Hawaiian Senator Daniel Inouye (ee-noh-oo-eh), and other celebrities. Nisei Week is a place and time for the Japanese American community to gather and show pride in their heritage.

Kenjinkai Picnic

If you had come to America 100 years ago from Japan, you might have gotten homesick. One way the Issei solved this problem was to stay in contact with other immigrants from their kenjinkai (kehn-jeen-kye), or home state in Japan. This helped people forget their loneliness for friends and family in Japan.

A very important community event started by Japanese Americans was the annual picnic, where people from different kenjinkai joined together in celebration. There were games and races for the children and adults. Singers, dancers, and bands playing Japanese music entertained everyone. Often, picnickers would get on stage and sing traditional folk songs.

People brought a packed lunch, called an *obento* (oh-behn-toh), to the picnic in a

special three-layer lacquered box set. The set was wrapped with a *furoshiki* (foo-roh-shee-kee), a scarf that had a Japanese design. Each layer was arranged in a pretty way. Some foods that were included were *onigiri* (oh-nee-gee-ree), rice balls); *tsuke-mono* (tsoo-keh-moh-noh), pickled vegetables; *teriyaki* (teh-ree-yah-kee) chicken; *sashimi* (sah-shee-mee), raw fish; *nishime* (nee-shee-meh), a one-pot vegetable dish; and *tempura* (tehm-poo-rah), deep-fried vegetables or seafood. The lunch was shared by friends and relatives. Kenjinkai picnics are still celebrated today.

MARTIAL ARTS

Sometimes when we think of art we think only about things that are on paper or things that we can make. We learned about an art that you can do! Martial arts are a fun and exciting way to get exercise and learn about yourself.

Karate

There are many types of *karate* (kah-rah-teh). Karate is more than 300 years old. It is a type of self-defense that uses punching, kicking, and moving. In karate you have to be quick. If someone throws a punch at you, you can dodge it or block it.

In karate you wear a clean, white gi and a belt, just like you do in judo. Each belt is a different color and stands for a different rank. The belt order is white, orange, yellow, blue, green, purple, brown, and black. In most groups, the black belt is the highest.

There are hundreds of stances in karate. We have drawn three basic stances (above) so you can see what they look like. They are the front stance, the back stance, and the horse.

In karate you spar. Sparring looks like fighting, but it is really a time to practice your moves. You wear special pads to protect your fists and head. You can also use blocks in karate. Blocks are ways to defend yourself with your arms and legs

HORSE STANCE

BACK STANCE

FRONT STANCE

that stop your opponent from striking or kicking you.

A *kata* (kah-tah) is several offensive and defensive movements put together. There are different katas, or forms. There is a kata for each belt. You need to know the kata and its meaning to pass each belt. Your kata needs to be perfect before you can test for the next higher belt.

Karate tournaments are held all across our country. At a tournament, you do your kata and then you free-spar in front of judges. The kata score can be from 0.0 to 10.0. Usually people score between 6.0 and 9.0. It is very unusual for people to get a 10, because that is a perfect score. If you do well you can get first, second, or third place.

We have told you about the exercise part, but we also want you to know that karate builds self-confidence and self-discipline. It teaches you to set goals and aim for them. The *sensei* (sen-say), or teacher, stresses these things with his or her students.

So, if you would like to develop self-confidence, have fun, practice movements, get exercise, and compete with an opponent, you should study karate. Karate is an exciting sport that uses the total mind and body.

Judo

Did you know that *judo* (joo-doh) can save your life? "Judo" means "the gentle way." It is a form of wrestling, but it is not used for fighting. Instead, it teaches you ways to escape from danger. In judo you learn how to fall safely so you won't get hurt or break any bones.

Chris Tucker

"Judo" means "the gentle way"

In judo you wear a *gi* (gee, with a hard "g"). It is a white uniform that looks like a jacket with loose-fitting pants. You use a colored belt to hold your gi together. The color of the belt stands for a different rank and is different depending on what school you go to. There are three levels in each color except black. The third level is *sankyu* (sahn-kyoo), the second level is *nikkyu* (nce-kyoo), and the first level is *ikkyu* (ee-kyoo). The highest color belt in judo is usually a black belt. There are ten *dans* (steps) in the black-belt rank, and ten is the highest. If you want to be a black belt, you have to show that you can do *Nage no Kata* (nah-geh noh kah-tah). These are a set of 15 different throws. You also have to show that you are a responsible person and that you will teach judo to other people.

When you begin to teach others judo, it is called *giri* (gee-ree), which means "obligation." You teach three things. These are self-defense, respect for nature, and discipline to your family, your friends, and the people in your community.

Students demonstrating judo

Many years ago, *samurai* (sah-moo-rye) warriors developed kendo to practice their sword-fighting skills. The first kendo fighters were men. Women fighters were called "naginatas."

Today, kendo is a competitive sport studied here in the United States by both men and women. "Kendo" means "the way of the sword." It is the Japanese style of fencing. A bamboo stick is used instead of a sword, and a steel grill is worn over the face like a mask. A shoulder and breast plate made of painted bamboo and arm coverings are used to protect the body. A long skirt is also worn, so you can't tell which way the fencer's feet are moving.

Today, judo is an event in the Olympic games. We think judo is a good way to defend yourself when a lot of people try to gang up on you. Learning about judo makes us want to sign up.

Kendo and Naginata

If you ever dreamed about being like Leonardo, the Ninja Turtle, you will love learning about *kendo* (kehn-doh) and *naginata* (nah-gee-nah-tah). Leonardo uses important skills he probably learned in kendo and naginata. These two martial arts require you to really concentrate on what you are doing. Both are forms of self-defense and are also practiced in competition. Martial arts are never used to hurt people.

Competing in a naginata tournament takes a lot of concentration, energy, and practice. Before a match, the participants bow to each other as a sign of respect.

We were lucky to meet and interview a woman who is an expert at naginata. Her name is Candy Tsutsui (tsoo-tsoo-ee). Mrs. Tsutsui competes in many matches and has practiced a lot to be a martial arts expert. Mrs. Tsutsui is really good at karate, but especially good at naginata. She uses some of the same techniques that the samurai warriors used in the old days. She has even been to Japan to compete in a tournament. For competi-tions, she dresses in a traditional outfit. Traditional protective gear can cost between $20,000 and $30,000, which is a lot of money! Luckily, there is a way to make gear out of fiberglass, which costs less. Mrs. Tsutsui has strong, proud feel-ings about her heritage. She showed us this by keeping the old traditions alive.

Kendo and naginata are fun martial arts to watch, especially because of the fierce sounds the competitors make. We think it is neat that these martial arts are used for self-defense and competition, and not for fighting. Anyone can take lessons. Maybe you would like to try it.

MUSIC AND DANCE

Another way you can learn many things about Japanese American culture is by listening to the music and watching the dances. In this section, you'll learn about some Japanese instruments, two Japanese American musical groups, and some Japanese ways of dancing and singing. This will give you a better understanding of the Japanese American heritage.

Taiko

Taiko (ty-koh) is an ancient form of drumming that was invented by a group of farmers long ago in Japan. The farmers used it to scare away any demons they thought would ruin their crops. After many years, it became a traditional folk art. Japanese Americans brought taiko to the United States.

Taiko consists of drums and percussion instruments that come in many shapes and sizes. The American-style taiko drums are made out of wine barrels and cowhides, while the other percussion instruments are made out of metal and wood. The music has a lot of different rhythms and patterns.

Vibrating drumbeats fill the air when a taiko group plays. The performances are very loud and exciting. They sound like thunder. The energy of the music adds to the excitement of the audience. The vibrations make you want to jump or pop and fly in the air.

There are many adult and children's taiko groups in Japanese American communities. Some of the authors of this book belong to a taiko group. People play the taiko drums because it is fun. They want to carry on the tradition so it won't be forgotten.

Shakuhachi

The tone of the *shakuhachi* (shah-koo-hah-chee) is very soothing and calming. It makes you feel like you're in the woods. The instrument is long and made out of a bamboo stick, with finger holes. You play it by blowing into it, like a flute. It originated in China, like most other Japanese instruments. The shakuhachi is used in traditional Japanese music and modern American music. A Japanese American jazz musician named Yutaka (yoo-tah-kah) plays the shakuhachi.

Koto

The word *koto* (koh-toh) originally meant "all kinds of string instruments." It is played like a guitar. The Japanese koto has 13 silk strings. The strings pass over moveable bridges. You pluck the strings with your finger tip and thumb or with a plectrum. A plectrum is like a large guitar pick. It is

Chris Tucker

Students demonstrating taiko drumming

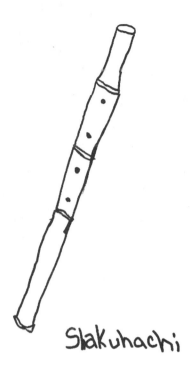

Shakuhachi

triangle-shaped and about the size of your palm. The koto is played flat on the floor, on your knees, or on a low table.

In the past, the koto was used only for classical Japanese music. But today, many modern Japanese American jazz groups use the koto when they play their music. The group Hiroshima uses this instrument. We liked the beautiful sounds of the koto.

Chris Tucker

Japanese women playing the koto

Samisen

Another traditional Japanese string instrument is the *samisen* (sah-mee-sehn). The first samisen was built in 1562. It is made of wood and has three strings and a wooden bridge. The covering is made of snakeskin. It looks almost like a banjo.

The samisen makes a high-pitched plucking sound. You play it like a guitar, sitting on your knees on the floor. It is played the traditional way, which is what you hear in classical Japanese music. It is also played the modern way, which is more of a jazz sound. It is played with a plectrum, which is like a guitar pick, or *bachi* (bah-chee), sticks used to strike the strings.

MUSICAL GROUPS

We don't have room to talk about all the different groups that use these instruments, but we can tell you about two groups: One World Taiko and Hiroshima. We have chosen these two groups because they are keeping Japanese American music alive.

One World Taiko

We were lucky to have Nancy Ozaki (oh-zah-kee) and Gary Tsujimoto (tsoo-jee-moh-toh) of One World Taiko perform for us. They take taiko drumming and combine the sounds of many cultures of America with the sounds of their ancestors. When they play, it is almost as if they know each other's thoughts.

Nancy Ozaki was born on Valentine's Day 1951 in Denver, Colorado, where she grew

Gary Tsujimoto and Nancy Ozaki of One World Taiko

Some of the authors playing taiko music

up. She is a second-generation Japanese American, or Nisei. As a teacher on a Navajo reservation, she was inspired by the Navajos' drums and music. She joined a Denver taiko group in 1976. In 1988, Ms. Ozaki moved to California and taught in an elementary school. She joined a taiko group there, too. This is where she met Gary Tsujimoto, a composer who also played taiko. Because they worked very well together, they started their own group. In 1989, they were married and moved to Pacifica, near San Francisco.

Mr. Tsujimoto was born in 1952 and is a third-generation Japanese America, or Sansei. He didn't become interested in his heritage until he was in college. He liked taiko because it combined his love of drums and karate with his culture. When he was in his twenties, he began playing taiko.

If you were to look for them now, you would find them in Florida working for Disney World at the EPCOT Center, sharing with others their love of taiko and their heritage. Ms. Ozaki and Mr. Tsujimoto are very

proud to be able to keep this part of their Japanese American heritage alive. We feel their name "One World Taiko" says it all— we all live in one world.

Hiroshima

Hiroshima (hee-roh-shee-mah) is a neat Sansei band that combines Japanese and American music together. They play music that sounds different to each person who listens to them. You might hear sounds of Latin, jazz, rock and roll, or something else. Best of all, this band plays Japanese American music that most kids like.

Hiroshima started in 1975. There are four main people in the group. Dan Kuramoto (koo-rah-moh-toh) is the leader of the band. He plays keyboards and woodwinds, like the shakuhachi. June Kuramoto plays the koto and samisen. Danny Yamamoto (yah-mah-moh-toh) is the drummer, and Johnny Mori (moh-ree) plays taiko. All four of them grew up in Los Angeles.

In the past, Hiroshima had a rough time being recognized, but now it is on its way

Bob Hsiang

Chris Tucker

to becoming a successful band. They are selling more albums than ever before and are winning awards for their music.

This group has many, many albums. In 1980, they received an award for Break-out Artist of the Year from *Performance Magazine*. "Winds of Change," a song from their second album, was nominated for a Grammy Award. We think it's awesome that Hiroshima blends old instruments with new ones and comes out with great sounds.

Singing

We sang songs every day during our workshop. Some of the songs were "Konnichiwa" (kohn-nee-chee-wah), "Harugakita" (hah-roo-gah-kee-tah), "Sakura" (sah-koo-rah), and "Usagi to Kame" (oo-sah-gee toh kah-meh). We can't put our voices in this book, so if you want to learn these and other songs, you can check out a book and a tape, both called *Japanese Children's Songs* (published by Nihonmachi Little Friends). It is put out by the Japanese American Museum in Los Angeles. These are available from the Japanese American Curriculum Project (1-800-874-2242), a nonprofit group that finds resources for teachers. You might also want to buy a tape of Hiroshima. If you're in Florida, stop in and see One World Taiko perform. In your own city you might be able to attend some folk dancing or a classical dance.

Dancing

Besides listening to Japanese American music, we also danced to it. There are two kinds of Japanese dancing, folk danc-

Sensei demonstrating the Tanko Bushi dance

ing and classical dancing. A folk dance is a people's dance. Men, women, and children all dance. You don't have to have a lot of training to do the folk dances. Festivals like Obon (the Festival of Lanterns to honor the dead) are times for folk dancing. Obon is explained earlier in this chapter.

Classical dance takes much longer to learn. Dancers take lessons and practice for many years. The classical dancer performs on a stage and wears lots of make-up and fancier kimonos than folk dancers wear. In both folk dancing and classical dancing, dancers use flowers, fans, hats, scarves,

Authors learning a dance for Obon

sticks, and *kachi-kachis* (kah-chee kah-chees). Kachi-kachis are wooden instruments that are clicked between two fingers like castanets.

Each dance has a story to go with it. We learned a dance called *Harugakita* (hah-roo-gah-kee-tah). The parts of this dance tell about the coming of spring in the mountains, plains, and meadows, when the flowers bloom and the birds return. Folk dances follow the same patterns of movements but can be changed by the number of steps. Individual dancers can choreograph classical dances so they can dance them the way they wish. You might see the same dance done differently depending on how the dancer wants to do it.

We all learned *Tanko Bushi* (tahn-koh boo-shee), a folk dance about coal mining. This is a circle dance. It is easier to learn a dance from watching someone else dance rather than reading about it, so you might want to ask a Japanese American person in your community to help you. Learning this dance was hard at first. It seemed slow, since it was hard to follow the patterns and stay together in a group. Some people even ran into each other by mistake. But it got easier as we went on. We all wore colorful *happi* (hah-pee), which are kimono coats, and *hachimakis* (hah-chee-mah-kees), which are headbands. In the future, we hope other people will learn the folk dances to carry on the tradition.

KIMONOS

During special celebrations and festivals you might see Japanese Americans wearing a *kimono* (kee-moh-noh). "Kimono" means "the thing worn." Both men and women wear kimonos. The kimono was first worn in Japan during the third or fourth century A.D.

Every kimono has an *obi* (oh-bee), a beautiful sash worn around the chest. The obi is about 15 feet long and 1 foot wide. You can tie an obi in many different ways. You can even show if you are married by the way it is tied.

Some people also wear *tabis* (tah-bees), which are like socks, *getas* (geh-tahs), which are wooden sandals that are raised up, or *zoris* (zoh-rees), which are flat sandals. Undergarments, like undershirts and half slips, are worn to protect the kimono,

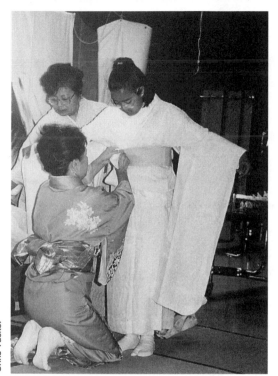

Chris Tucker

Learning how to tie an obi

THE TEA CEREMONY

In the United States, Japanese Americans enjoy drinking tea, but few do the tea ceremony in their homes. It was started by Buddhist monks in Japan, who sometimes used the tea for medicine. This tradition is being carried on by some Japanese American cultural organizations. In fact, you might be able to have someone from such an organization come to your school or group to demonstrate the tea ceremony for you. Some Issei and Nisei women came and did a tea ceremony for us.

The tea ceremony is performed in a very careful, special way. It can last from half an hour to an hour and a half, depending on how many people are served. First, a little powdered tea is put into the tea bowl. Then hot water is poured into the bowl, just enough for three or four sips. The tea is stirred with a bamboo brush. The tea looks green and foamy and tastes like hot water with a little spice in it.

which can be very expensive. Hairpieces and handbags are sometimes used as accessories. It can take as long as an hour to get dressed in a kimono.

Although many Japanese Americans have kimonos, they wear them only for special festivals like Girls' Day and Obon, a festival to remember the dead. Others wear *yukata* (yoo-kah-tah), cotton summer kimonos. They also wear kimonos for special occasions like tea ceremonies and folk dancing. Kimonos are so beautiful it's no wonder that some are displayed in museums. If you have a chance, attend a Japanese American festival to see these colorful kimonos.

Chris Tucker

Performing the special tea ceremony

The server then gives each guest a bowl of tea. The server moves carefully and calmly. Tea ceremonies are never noisy.

When the guests drink the tea, they cup their hands around the bowl. There are no handles on the bowl, and each tea bowl is different. Part of the pleasure of the tea ceremony comes from the feel of the warm bowl.

We each made a tea bowl in art class. It took a lot of concentration. The bowls didn't turn out exactly the way we wanted, but somehow they looked good. They were a lot of different shapes and sizes. Before we made our pottery we planned and thought about the style, design, and color. It was really fun to see how the bowls turned out after we glazed and fired them. We wanted to go home and drink some tea from our bowls.

ARCHITECTURE

In many places across America you can see examples of Japanese architecture. Americans have taken Japanese styles and used them in all kinds of buildings, from restaurants to shopping malls.

In many cities throughout the United States, you can find a Japanese American cultural center that is almost like a small town. Some examples of these are the International District (Seattle, Washington), Japan Town (San Francisco, California), Sakura Square (Denver, Colorado), and Little Tokyo (Los Angeles, California). Japanese Americans sponsor festivals and celebrations at these centers and people of all different heritages come and enjoy them.

Japanese styles of architecture can be found all over the U.S.

Chris Tucker

If you visit one of these cultural centers, you will see the influence of Japanese architecture in the roofs, gates, doors, and windows. Often you can see a *torii* (toh-ree-ee), a wooden gateway with two columns and a cross bar on top. The ends of the cross bar arch upward. In these Japanese American cultural centers, you can find Japanese restaurants, churches, markets, gift shops, travel agencies, and barber shops.

In the restaurants you might be taken into a room with *tatami* (tah-tah-mee) mats on the floor. These mats are made from rice straw and smell like sweet grass. You take off your shoes before entering this room. You eat at a low table and sit on flat cushions instead of chairs. Some restaurants also have *shoji* (shoh-jee), sliding doors, that look like windows with white squares of paper in them. Light can come through but you can't see through the paper. Keep your eyes open and you will see many examples of Japanese architecture all across America.

JAPANESE GARDENS

Japanese gardens are different from the gardens or flowers that many people have in their backyards.

The rocks, fountains, and plants used in Japanese gardens in America are not the same as those used in Japan because our climate is different. Most Japanese Americans do not have a Japanese garden in their backyards but many other Americans are carrying on this tradition. These gardens are often a blend of Japanese and American styles of landscaping.

If you were to take a tour of special gardens in your city, you might see several that

A Japanese-style garden in Colorado

have been influenced by the Japanese style. One of the neat things about the many cultures in our country is that Americans of all backgrounds pick up parts of other people's heritages and make them a part of their own traditions.

If you want to see a Japanese garden, go to a botanical garden near your home or visit a Japanese cultural center. Some well-known Japanese gardens are:

Denver Botanical Gardens in Denver, Colorado

Golden Gate Park in San Francisco, Caifornia

Japanese Garden in the Arboretum in Seattle, Washington

The Japanese Garden in Portland, Orgon

Japanese Tea Garden in San Mateo, Caifornia

Huntington Library Art Collection Botanical Garden in San Marino, California

National Arboretum in Washington, D.C.

IKEBANA

Ikebana (ee-keh-bah-nah) is the art of flower arranging. Although it started in Japan in the 1400s, today some Japanese Americans and other Americans still arrange and display flowers using the traditional techniques and styles. During our workshop, we were given a lesson in ikebana, and we made our own flower arrangements. They looked beautiful displayed next to our tea bowls and on the tables for our celebration dinner. We loved the

way ikebana made us feel. It can be very relaxing and comforting.

The flowers you use in ikebana depend on the season. Each flower or plant has a special place in the arrangement and means something different. The tallest branches or flowers stand for the heavens. The middle ones stand for the people, and the lowest stand for the earth. It is important to keep the design simple.

There are ten different schools of ikebana but only four basic styles of ikebana. They are *Rikka* (ree-kah), which is the oldest style, *Moribana* (moh-ree-bah-nah), the natural style, *Shoka* (shoh-kah), a sleek and delicate style, and *Nageire* (nah-geh-ee-reh), a more casual style.

Chris Tucker

The art of flower arranging is called ikebana

Ikebana helps us appreciate the beauty and wonder of nature. Though ikebana looks very simple to do, it's not. To actually create one of the styles takes a lot of practice and hard work.

Many cities in the U.S. have places that offer ikebana lessons. Japanese festivals in America sometimes have examples of ikebana on display. Many Americans enjoy ikebana as a hobby.

SUMI-E

Sumi-e (soo-mee-eh) is Japanese ink painting. How is sumi-e different from other kinds of painting? One difference is that the artists use ink that they make themselves. To do this they use an inkstone and an ink stick called a *sumi* (soo-mee) stick. The sumi stick is made out of carbon from burnt pine.

Before beginning to paint, there are strict rules to follow:

1. Sit up straight.
2. Don't chew gum.
3. Put one hand on the paper while you hold the brush with your other hand.
4. Get your mind ready to paint.

The basic colors of sumi-e are black and white. Black ink is painted on white paper. Backgrounds are not painted in. The painter considers the white area as the background and it has special meaning in sumi-e.

When you are first learning sumi-e, you

paint simple things like grass. Then you are ready to paint harder things like flowers. With just a few brushstrokes, a picture is complete. Each stroke is important to the picture.

You can find sumi-e paintings in homes, restaurants, and museums. Some Japanese Americans create sumi-e art. If you have a chance, watch someone give a demonstration on sumi-e. You will be amazed at the picture that will appear with just a few strokes of the brush. Sumi-e uses the same brushstrokes as calligraphy.

CALLIGRAPHY

Calligraphy is the art of fine handwriting. Japanese calligraphy, called *shodo* (shoh-

Chris Tucker

Japanese calligraphy

JAPANESE AMERICAN ARTISTS

There are many Japanese American artists all across America. We only have room to tell about a few. These artists have blended techniques from their heritage with American ways and developed their own style of artwork. These artists are sort of like pioneers. Read on to see how art became a lifestyle for six famous Japanese American artists.

Yuzuru Henry Sugimoto (1900–1990)

Yuzuru Sugimoto (yoo-zoo-roo soo-gee-moh-toh) was a very devoted painter and loved what he did. He did not let anything stop him from painting. In fact, during his time in the internment camps, he

doh), uses the same ink, paper, and brushes that are used for sumi-e painting, which you just read about.

Learning calligraphy is not easy. It takes a lot of time, patience, and practice. You have to put everything else aside and concentrate on what you are doing. It takes many years to learn the characters in the Japanese language and how to use the brush.

If you visit a Japanese American cultural center you might see examples of calligraphy.

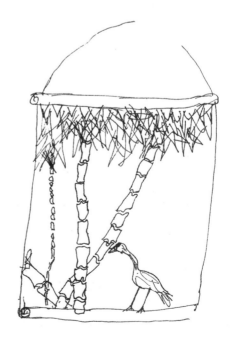

painted on bed sheets, fruit packing canvas, and any other material he could find.

Over the years, Mr. Sugimoto did oil paintings of European scenes, designed fabric, and made block prints that showed his Japanese heritage. His work has been displayed in the Smithsonian Institute in Washington D.C., UCLA Wright Art Gallery in Los Angeles, and in the International Gallery in New York.

We enjoyed looking at Mr. Sugimoto's bright and beautiful art work and know he will not be forgotten. He had a long and wonderful life of 90 years. He died in 1990.

Hisako Hibi (1907–1991)

Hisako Hibi (hee-sah-koh hee-bee) once said, "Painting knows no color or race. If I want a better house, I can paint one. If I want a road, I can paint a road. And if I want to see beauty I can see the clouds go by."

Mrs. Hibi loved her grandma because she taught Mrs. Hibi to look for beauty in her life and to work hard. She was married in 1930 and painted lots of things in the thirties that were lost when her family was put in the internment camp in 1942. After the war her pictures changed and were dark and scary. Over the years they became lighter as she remembered what her Grandma had taught her. In fact, her work done in the 1950s was very light and transparent. She told how her art brought back her memories as colors.

Today you can see her art displayed in galleries across our nation, such as the Japanese American National Museum in Los Angeles.

Mine Okubo (b. 1912)

Mine Okubo (mee-neh oh-koo-boh) uses painting as a tool to find truth and beauty. Her work is very beautiful and colorful. It is bright and bold. She became famous when she was in her late twenties and did two solo shows in 1940 and 1941.

While in an internment camp, she taught art classes. After the war she became an illustrator for magazines including *Fortune*, *Life*, and the *Saturday Review*. Her work has changed over the years from stiff abstractions to still life with strong colors and form.

Ms. Okubo has also written a book called *Citizen 13660* that tells about her camp experiences. Ms. Okubo has had many exhibits in the past, including one in the National Museum of Women in the Arts in Washington D.C. in 1991.

Matsumi Mike Kanemitsu (1922–1992)

Matsumi Kanemitsu (maht-soo-mee kah-neh-meet-soo) was born in Ogden, Utah in 1922. He served in the U.S. Army in World War II. After the war he decided to become an artist. He was an abstract painter who also made prints using metal plates.

Mr. Kanemitsu's artwork is much different than other abstract painters because it uses traditional Japanese sumi-e styles and modern American ideas together. This truly expresses the Japanese American heritage. He once said, "When a tiger dies it leaves its fur. When a person dies he leaves his name." We are also glad Mr. Kanemitsu left his name on his beautiful and unique art.

Ruth Asawa (b. 1926)

Ruth Asawa (ah-sah-wah) was both unlucky and lucky. She was unlucky because she was put in an internment camp. She was lucky because Tom Okamoto (oh-kah-moh-toh), who had been a Disney artist, taught kids in her camp to draw and do art activities. She was born in 1926 in California and put into an internment camp in Rohwer, Arkansas.

After her camp experience, she studied to be an art teacher at Milwaukee State College. She believes that you can teach children values through art and find the

answers to your problems doing art. She has worked with many different kinds of sculptures and has also done graphic arts.

Ruth Asawa has had many exhibits in cities across our nation including New York, Boston, and San Francisco. She has been hired to do many large sculptures and fountains by different cities and companies. Keep your eyes open because someday you might see one of her big sculptures right in front of you.

MUSEUMS

If you want to learn more about Japanese American culture and art you might want to visit a museum while you and your family are traveling. Some well-known museums include:

Bishop Museum in Honolulu, Hawaii
The Japanese American National
  Museum in Los Angeles, California
Morikami (moh-ree-kah-mee) Museum
  in Del Ray Beach, Florida
Wing Luke Museum in Seattle,
  Washington

The Japanese American Historical
  Society in San Francisco, California
Smithsonian National Museum of
  American History in Washington,
  D.C.

FAMOUS FIRSTS AND HEROES

This chapter is on the brave and bold
Men and women, young and old,
Who have made our country a better place.
They have worked hard for the human race.

In this chapter, you will find a lot of people who are famous and have been the first to do something. We see them as heroes. These Japanese Americans have been through a lot and have worked hard to overcome problems. Even during bad times, these people have made good things happen. With their courage and determination, they made a difference in many people's lives. Whether you want to be a teacher, a lawyer, a writer, or something else, these heroes' stories will inspire you.

We found in writing this chapter that there aren't a lot of books around that tell about famous Japanese Americans. We decided to write about as many Japanese Americans as possible to make sure these people are not forgotten. Some of the biographies are long, but many are short so

we could include as many as possible. The biographies are in order by date of birth. We did not have the space to include a biography on everyone, so at the end of the chapter we included a list of other famous firsts.

FEATURED BIOGRAPHIES

Takino Washimi Takamatsu (1886–1985)

In 1971, Mrs. Takino Washimi Takamatsu (tah-kee-noh wah-shee-mee tah-kah-mah-tsoo) received the Fifth-Class Order of Sacred Treasure from the Japanese government for her efforts in sharing the Japanese culture. She was the first woman in Colorado to receive the medal, which is given to naturalized American citizens from Japan. She taught people how to play the koto, do

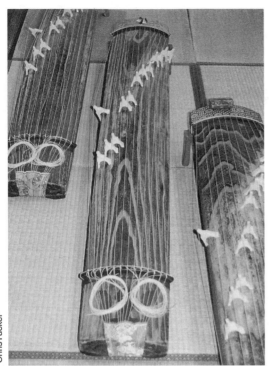

Chris Tucker

Mrs. Takamatsu taught people how to play the koto

flower arranging, and perform the tea ceremony until she was in her nineties. Mrs. Takamatsu died December 29, 1985, at the age of 99.

Mrs. Takamatsu was born on April 24, 1886, at the Kokutaiji (koh-koo-ty-jee) Temple in Hiroshima, Japan. Her father was a Zen (zehn) priest descended from samurai warriors. Mrs. Takamatsu got a good education when she was a child. Her father died when she was only seven, so Mrs. Takamatsu and her mother moved from the temple. Unfortunately, the person handling her father's will stole their money. When she grew older, Mrs. Takamatsu became a teacher so she could support her mom and herself.

Years later, Mrs. Takamatsu met Saburo (sah-boo-roh) Takamatsu. They got married and left for California where Mr. Takamatsu had already started a peach orchard and a strawberry farm. Then Mr. Takamatsu died of lung cancer. After her husband's death, Mrs. Takamatsu continued to teach in Colusa, California, and raise her four children. When World War II began, the Japanese School was closed and a curfew was ordered. When Executive Order 9066 was posted on a telephone pole on their block, it instructed the Japanese Isseis and Niseis to leave the area within a week.

Home in the internment camp was one room in a wooden barrack with brick floors. The only source of heat during the cold winter days was a pot-belly stove. Mrs. Takamatsu was ordered not to teach the Japanese language, so she taught knitting instead. At the end of World War II, Mrs. Takamatsu left for Denver. There, she found work re-weaving Oriental rugs at Sarkisian's Oriental Rug Shop. She worked there until she was in her eighties. She kept on teaching at the Japanese Language School at the Denver Buddhist Temple into her nineties.

John Aiso (1909–1987)

Imagine you want to be the student body president or a leader in your neighborhood, but all the people who want the same thing are different from you. You might feel scared, or you might stand up for yourself and make them see that you are just as smart as everyone else. Well, that is what Mr. John Aiso (eye-soh) did.

Courtesy of Archie A. Miyatake

Mr. John Aiso

ation because he was a good student. He then went to Harvard Law School and joined a New York law firm after graduation. In 1939, Mr. Aiso went back to Los Angeles. During World War II, he was the head of military intelligence and retired as a colonel. Earl Warren, who was then the governor of California, appointed Mr. Aiso to be municipal court judge in Los Angeles in 1953. He was the first Japanese American to be a superior court judge on the mainland.

Sadly, in 1987 Mr. Aiso was killed by a mugger at a gas station.

Minoru Yasui (1916–1988)

Would you stand up for your rights as an American citizen? Well, that is exactly what

Mr. Aiso was born in Los Angeles in 1909. He started standing up for himself at age 13. He went to Hollywood High School and decided he wanted to be student body president. Lots of people in the school thought he was really smart and voted for him. After he won, the parents in the school caused a lot of trouble by saying that he wasn't American because he was of Japanese American heritage. The principal cancelled all student government activities until Mr. Aiso graduated, because he felt that if Mr. Aiso couldn't be president, no one could.

After graduating from Hollywood High School, Mr. Aiso studied for one year in Tokyo, Japan. Then he entered Brown University at age 17, graduated with good grades, and was chosen to speak at gradu-

Chris Tucker

Statue honoring Mr. Minoru Yasui

Minoru Yasui (mee-noh-roo yah-soo-ee) did.

Minoru Yasui was born in Hood River, Oregon, on October 19, 1916. He was the third son of Masuo (mah-soo-oh) and Shizuyo (shee-zoo-yoh) Yasui. He and his five brothers and three sisters were Nisei, or second generation.

Mr. Yasui had wanted to become a lawyer ever since he was a kid, and his wish came true. He got his law degree in 1939. Mr. Yasui also received a second lieutenant commission from the U.S. Army Reserve. Then he worked in Chicago, where he was employed by the Japanese Consulate. After the war broke out, Mr. Yasui decided to resign. Soon afterward, he received Army orders to report to active duty, but when he went to report, he wasn't wanted. Since the Army didn't want him at that time, he decided to open a law office in Portland, Oregon.

In 1942, a curfew was put into effect. It ordered all Japanese Americans to stay in their houses or be at work from 8:00 p.m. to 6:00 a.m. No Japanese Americans were allowed to come out until the morning. Mr. Yasui did not follow this curfew order, because he believed in standing up for his rights. He thought that the order to stay inside was stupid because he was an American citizen. Just because he was a different race, the government thought he was a spy.

A policeman arrested Mr. Yasui, and the government made him pay $5,000 and sent him to a county jail for one year. While he was in jail, he tried to appeal his case, saying he didn't do anything wrong, but he had to stay in jail. Mr. Yasui's appeal was directed to the U.S. Supreme Court. The U.S. Supreme Court finally decided to overturn the case against him.

After Mr. Yasui got out of jail, he continued to be a lawyer. He always tried to help his community. He changed a lot of people's lives for the better.

Tsuyako "Sox" Kitashima (b. 1918)

You can't erase the events of the past, but you can keep them from happening again. This is one belief that Ms. Tsuyako Kitashima (tsoo-yah-koh kee-tah-shee-mah) tells others. Better known as "Sox" Kitashima, she is a civil rights activist. That means she stands up for the rights of her people. In fact, Ms. Kitashima has stood up not only for her rights as a Japanese American, but also for the rights of people of other heritages as well.

Ms. Kitashima began her fight for civil rights in 1979. She spoke to the members of Congress who were holding hearings about Japanese Americans who were held in internment camps during World War II.

Takeshi Nakayama

Ms. Tsuyako "Sox" Kitashima (second from left) with friends at the Department of Justice

From 1979 to 1989, many Japanese American groups worked hard to pass a bill called the American Civil Liberties Act to help people understand how unfair it was to put Japanese Americans in the camps. Ms. Kitashima worked very hard on this bill. She collected over 25,000 letters to take to Washington, D.C. She also tried to talk to as many people as she could in Congress to get the bill passed. After three tries, it did pass in 1988.

Yoshiko Uchida (b. 1921)

How would you like it if many, many guards were always watching you, making sure you didn't do anything wrong? What would you do? Would you write about it? Well, that's what Yoshiko Uchida (yoh-shee-kah oo-chee-da) did. She wrote about her experience in a WWII internment camp.

Ms. Uchida, a Nisei, is the first Japanese American to write full-time for young readers. Her books help students and even adults understand what it was like for her living in Topaz, an internment camp in Utah. She named this book *Journey to Topaz* (New York: Charles Scribner, 1971). She wrote her first book when she was little. It was written on brown wrapping paper.

Yoshiko Uchida was born in Alameda, California, and grew up in the 1930s. In 1942, she and her family were put in an internment camp. Ms. Uchida saw many sad things there. There was not enough food, and some people died because of this.

One of the helpful things Ms. Uchida did in the camp was to volunteer to teach school along with other people, so the children could keep learning. The whole time Ms. Uchida was in Topaz, she kept a journal about the sad and happy moments of her life.

When Ms. Uchida grew older, she decided that she wanted to write stories about being Japanese American. She has written many books for young readers about Japan and Japanese American children in the United States. She wants Japanese American children to understand and appreciate their heritage. She also wants all children to know that everyone should be treated the same no matter what.

Courtesy of *Tozai Times*

Lt. Col. Ellison Onizuka

Ellison S. Onizuka (1946–1986)

Lots of kids hope that one day they might fly in a rocket to the moon, or travel to the stars like in *Star Trek*. Going up in space was also a dream for Mr. Ellison S. Onizuka (oh-nee-zoo-kah), the first Japanese American astronaut.

Mr. Onizuka's sisters remember him as a rascal when he was young. He liked to take things apart around the house. One New Year's Eve, he found an unlit firecracker, called a "roman candle," and took it to the basement to see how it worked. He had seen adults light this type of firecracker before, so he lit it himself. Upstairs, there were loud thumps hitting the floor, as the candle smoked and exploded. Panicking, his family ran downstairs and found him testing his first rocket. As Mr. Onizuka grew up, he wanted more and more to be an astronaut.

He was born on June 24, 1946. Mr. Onizuka had two older sisters and one younger brother. Since Mr. Onizuka was the first-born son, he was treated differently from his brother and sisters. He had more chores to do than his brother, and he had to work in his father's store and in the coffee fields. Mr. Onizuka had a good imagination. In fact, it was so good, he would take his brother for rides in a cardboard box that he pretended was a car.

Mr. Onizuka attended elementary and high schools in Hawaii. Then went to the University of Colorado. He went to Vance Air Force base in Oklahoma for his astronaut training, which started in 1978.

The first space flight that Mr. Onizuka went on was the *Discovery* flight. There

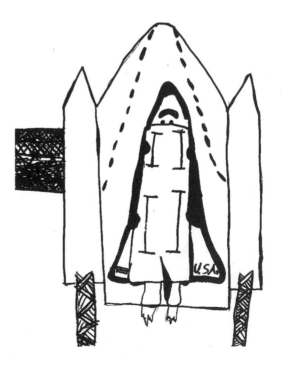

were five men on board on January 24, 1985. He felt sad because he could not tell people about the flight because it was top secret. One of his friends asked him how high he was above the earth, but he couldn't even tell that. He told his friend, "Next question." That's how top secret it was.

On January 28, 1986, Ellison Onizuka went on another very important space flight. The control room started the countdown. 10 . . . 9 . . . 8 . . . 7 . . . 6 . . . 5 . . . 4 . . . 3 . . . 2 . . . 1 . . 0 . . . . Blast off! Only seconds after its takeoff, something went wrong in the engines and the *Challenger* exploded, killing all seven astronauts inside.

We think that Mr. Onizuka was a brave man for going on the *Challenger* shuttle, and we are sad that he died at such a young age. Mr. Onizuka was very close to many people, and they will always remember him. Americans will always remember Mr. Ellison Onizuka and the *Challenger* tragedy of 1986.

Kristi Yamaguchi (b. 1971)

"When I'm skating, I feel like I can express myself. I feel free." This is a comment you might hear when you talk to the first Japanese American woman ever to win an Olympic gold medal for ice skating.

Miss Kristi Tsuya Yamaguchi (tsoo-yah yah-mah-goo-chee) was born on July 12, 1971, in Hayward, California. She grew up in Fremont, which is in the San Francisco area. Some people don't know that she was born and raised in California, and think that she is from Japan. In fact, she hardly speaks any Japanese at all. Her father

Tana J. Monji

Miss Kristi Yamaguchi

is a dentist and her mother is a medical secretary. Both of her parents spent time in the internment camps during World War II. Miss Yamaguchi is a fourth-generation Japanese American, or Yonsei.

When Miss Yamaguchi was born, she had club feet. The term "club feet" comes from the clublike look of the feet, because of

an inward and downward turning of each foot. She had to wear corrective shoes to straighten her feet out.

At age five, she started to take skating lessons. She was eight years old when she entered her first competition. The next year she started getting up at 4:00 a.m. so she could skate for several hours before school. She did this because she was determined to win competitions.

In 1985, she was paired with Rudi Galindo, another skater. They won fifth place at the National Junior Championships. In 1989, Miss Yamaguchi won two medals, a gold medal in pairs competition and a second place in the singles competition at the Nationals. At the World Championships in Paris, she was the sixth-best singles skater in the world.

Miss Kristi Yamaguchi was 20 years old when she won a gold medal in figure skating for the United States in the 1992 Winter Olympics. After she won this medal, she won her second World Championship, becoming the first female skater to successfully defend her world title since Ms. Peggy Fleming did it in 1968.

Besides skating, Miss Yamaguchi likes to play tennis, go rollerblading, read, dance, and cheer for the San Francisco 49ers football team. She attends the Alameda Buddhist Temple. She is popular wherever she goes. Because she is so famous, she has become a hero to many kids, and adults, too. She has been honored by the San Francisco Asian Chamber of Commerce, a national businesswomen's association, the Pan Asian National Chamber of Commerce, and the Japanese American Citizens League.

SHORT BIOGRAPHIES

Joseph Heco (1837–1897)

Mr. Hikozo Hamada (hee-koh-zoh ham-mah-dah), later known as Joseph Heco, was only 13 years old when he got lost in a big storm on the sea. For fifty days, his boat drifted toward America.

An American ship rescued Mr. Hamada and the other sailors, and took them to the United States. Mr. Hamada met a lot of people here. One of them was the president of the United States, Abraham Lincoln!

Mr. Hamada became a citizen of the United States in 1858 and changed his name to Jospeh Heco. He was the first Japanese person to become an American citizen, and he did it almost one hundred years before any other Japanese were allowed to become citizens.

Many years later he returned to Japan to work for the United States and Japanese governments as an interpreter.

Fred Wada (b. 1908)

Have you ever dreamed of being a millionaire? Mr. Fred Wada (wah-dah) is. Mr. Wada was born in California in 1908. He is famous for advising and working for the Olympic committee.

When he was young, Mr. Wada had to go to Japan to live with his grandparents. He came back to the United States when he

Courtesy of Archie A. Miyatake

Mr. Fred Wada with his wife in a Nisei parade

was nine. At age 12, he was forced out of his home to make room for his younger brothers and sisters. When he was 15, he quit school and got a job delivering milk. When he had saved enough money, Mr. Wada started his own fruit stand, which later became a chain of produce stores across America.

In 1959, Mr. Wada got a letter from Japan asking him to help get votes from other countries, so that the Olympic Games could be held in Japan. He made a deal with Mexico that if Japan could host the 1964 Olympics, he would help Mexico host the 1968 Olympics. The deal worked, and both countries got what they wanted. The 1964 Olympics were held in Tokyo, and the 1968 Olympics were held in Mexico City.

Mr. Wada was an advisor to Mexico and Japan for several years. Later, he got interested in fund-raising for a nursing home. Mr. Wada gave $1 million to charity. He has donated large amounts of money to the poor.

Mr. Wada is a perfect example of a self-made man, a man who did things on his own.

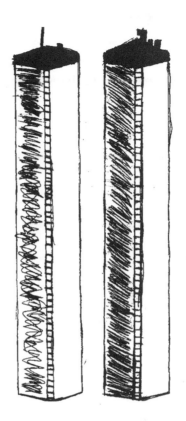

Minoru Yamasaki (1912–1986)

If you have been to Los Angeles, New York, Detroit, St. Louis, Seattle, or Saudi Arabia, you have probably seen amazing buildings designed by Minoru Yamasaki (mee-noh-roo yah-mah-sah-kee). He was a famous Japanese American architect who designed more than three hundred buildings.

Mr. Yamasaki was born in 1912 in Seattle, Washington. He graduated from the University of Washington in 1939 with a degree in architecture. In 1945, he moved to Detroit and became head designer for an architectural company. The first important building he designed was the airport terminal in St. Louis, for which he received his first award. Two of the most famous buildings that Mr. Yamasaki designed are the Twin Towers of the World Trade Center in New York City. Mr. Yamasaki won many awards for his great architecture. He died in 1986.

John Naka (b. 1914)

Have you ever seen the miniature Japanese trees called bonsai? You might have wondered how they are shaped or who makes them. Mr. John Naka (nah-kah) teaches the art of bonsai all over the United States, India, Japan, and many other countries. Mr. Naka has devoted his life to keeping the art of bonsai alive.

Mr. Naka was born in Colorado and studied bonsai in Japan. At age 21, he moved back to Colorado and started farming in

Courtesy of Tozai Times

Bonsai tree

Brighton. He later married Alice Mizunaga (mee-zoo-nah-gah) and moved to Los Angeles, where he began teaching bonsai.

Mr. Naka has a display of his trees in the United States National Arboretum in Washington, D.C. An arboretum is like a big garden that people can look at or visit. Mr. Naka is so famous for the art of bonsai that he is called "Mr. Bonsai."

Mike Masaoka (1915–1991)

Mike Masaoka (mah-sah-oh-kah) never gave up on fighting for Japanese Americans' civil rights, which are the rights guaranteed to all citizens of the United States. They include speaking and living freely.

Mr. Masaoka was born on October 15, 1915, in Fresno, California. When he was one year old, his family moved to Salt Lake City and opened a grocery store. His father died when Mr. Masaoka was nine. As he grew older, he wanted people to know how much he loved America. He wanted them to know that although he looked Japanese, he was an American.

He joined the the Japanese American Citizens League (JACL). Members of the JACL went around the country telling everybody that Japanese Americans were like any other people. Japanese Americans play, sing, and eat just like anybody else. When the government found out that Mr. Masaoka was one of the leaders of the JACL, they put him in jail. This happened to him many times before World War II, and then he joined the U.S. Army.

While Mr. Masaoka fought for the United States in Europe, his family was sent to

Courtesy of Tozai Times

Mr. Mike Masaoka

Manzanar Internment Camp. He won the Distinguished Service Cross award for bravery.

Yuri Kochiyama (b. 1921)

Yuri Kochiyama (yoo-ree koh-chee-yah-mah) is a human rights protector. She became a human rights protector because she was put in internment camps during World War II. While she was in the camps, she felt separated and discriminated against. Those feelings made her want to help others.

During the 1960s, Mrs. Kochiyama moved to Harlem, New York. She wanted to help her neighbors who were African American fight for their civil rights. She helped other people get jobs, transportation, and education.

An important time in Mrs. Kochiyama's life was when she met Malcolm X. He was an African American leader who fought for the rights of African Americans. She joined Malcolm X in fighting for the rights of all different races.

Mrs. Kochiyama still lives in Harlem and is still an activist fighting for the rights of all races.

Sadao Munemori (1923–1945)

Sadao Munemori (sah-dah-oh moo-neh-moh-ree) was the first Nisei to get a Congressional Medal of Honor for being a hero in World War II. This medal is the highest honor in the U.S. military.

Mr. Munemori was born in 1923. He joined the Army right after he finished high school. He asked to be moved to a com-

bat unit and joined the 442nd Regimental Combat Team, a troop made up of Japanese Americans. He was awarded his Medal of Honor after he died from diving on a grenade to save the lives of two other American soldiers on April 5, 1945. He was 22 years old.

Sayuri Harami (b. 1925)

Sayuri Harami (sah-yoo-ree hah-rah-mee) was one of the first Japanese American women to be hired by the California Institute of Technology's Jet Propulsion Laboratory (JPL). JPL is the center for unmanned space science. "Unmanned" means there are no people on board the spacecraft.

When Mrs. Harami worked on the space program, she worked with computers for the Ranger, Surveyor, Mariner, and Viking space projects. These were spacecraft that were sent to study the surfaces of the the moon and the planets Mercury, Venus, and Mars.

Later, Mrs. Harami transferred to work in another area of research at JPL. She says she

did her most important work at this time. She helped study chromosomes.

Mrs. Harami was born in 1925 in Long Beach, California. She is a Nisei. She is now retired and lives in California. She enjoys raising dogs and traveling around the country showing them. Mrs. Harami has shown us that women can do anything they want when they set their minds to it.

Patsy Takemoto Mink (b. 1927)

Patsy Takemoto (tah-keh-moh-toh) Mink is a very important woman in Hawaii. She was the first Japanese American woman lawyer in Hawaii. She is also the first Nisei woman to be elected to the U.S. House of Representatives.

Ms. Mink was born on the island of Maui and lived most of her life in Hawaii. She got her law degree from the University of Hawaii in 1951. She worked very hard helping with election campaigns during the 1950s. It was an exciting day in 1964 when Ms. Mink was elected to the House of Representatives. She fought for women to be recognized for what they do, for child-care laws, and for non-discrimination, so everybody could get a chance to do the things they want.

Dr. Paul I. Terasaki (b. 1929)

Everyone was in shock after the partial meltdown of the Chernobyl nuclear reactor in the former Soviet Union in 1986. After the accident, Dr. Paul I. Terasaki (teh-rah-sah-kee) traveled to Russia to work with the people who were suffering from radiation sickness. Radiation sickness is caused

Courtesy of Archie A. Miyatake

Dr. Paul Terasaki

by nuclear radiation. The doctors who rushed to Chernobyl risked their lives to help the sick people. Some of the procedures that were used to help people wouldn't have happened if it weren't for Dr. Terasaki. He and the people who worked with him discovered the art of tissue-typing needed for organ transplants.

Dr. Terasaki is a doctor in Los Angeles. He is a scientist in the special medical field of matching blood types. He works to make certain you get the right blood when you need it. His job is important, because if you get the wrong blood type you could get very sick.

Dr. Terasaki is the winner of many awards, such as the Netherlands Red Cross Medal, the Modern Medicine Award for Dis-

tinguished Achievement, UCLA's Distinguished Achievement Award, and the American Society of Clinical Pathologists Philip Levine Award.

Dr. Terasaki is famous because he cares for people all around the world. He displayed this when he helped the people of Chernobyl.

Edison Uno (1929–1976)

Edison Uno (oo-noh) was a fighter for justice. His lifelong goal was to make the U.S. government admit it had made a mistake when it put Japanese Americans into interment camps.

Mr. Uno was born on October 19, 1929. In 1942, his father was arrested and his family was ordered to go to living quarters at the Santa Anita Race Track in California. After the war, Mr. Uno returned to live in California. There, he finished his education and married Rosalind Kidd.

In 1972, the U.S. government removed Title II of the McCarran International Security Act of 1950. This act said you could put people in jail without a trial if they were suspected spies. Mr. Uno worked hard to overturn this act so it would no longer be legal.

On December 24, 1976, Mr. Uno's heart failed and he died. It seemed that all of his work for the apology to the interned Japanese Americans had been in vain, but it turned out that he had done a good job. In 1984, the U.S. government formally apologized for its mistake in sending the Japanese Americans to internment camps during World War II.

Courtesy of Tozai Times

Mr. Norman Mineta (center) with supporters

Courtesy of Tozai Times

Mr. Noriyuki "Pat" Morita in The Karate Kid

Norman Mineta (b. 1931)

Have you ever dreamed of being mayor of your town? In 1971, Mr. Mineta (mee-neh-tah) was elected mayor of San Jose, California. This made him the first Japanese American mayor of a major city in the continental United States.

Norman Mineta was born in San Jose on November 12, 1931. When he was a child, he and his family were forced out of their home and sent to an internment camp.

When he got out of the internment camp, he got his high school diploma and then went to college. He earned a Bachelor of Science degree in business at the University of California at Berkeley in 1953. After that, Mr. Mineta went on duty for the U.S. Army as a military intelligence officer.

When he got out of the army, Mr. Mineta became involved in community activities. In 1962, he joined the San Jose Human Relations Commission. It was his first public post. Mr. Mineta also became a member of the San Jose City Council in 1967.

Noriyuki "Pat" Morita (b. 1932)

Many people dream of one day becoming a famous actor. After years of hard work as a computer operator, disc jockey, actor, and comedian, Mr. Noriyuki Morita (no-ree-yoo-kee moh-ree-tah) became a big hit in the movie *The Karate Kid*. Kids all over began to say lines from the movie, like, "Wax on, wax off."

Mr. Morita, better known as "Pat," was born in 1932 in Iselton, California. During his childhood he overcame a spinal disease and living in an internment camp. This taught him to be brave and not to give up.

As an actor, Mr. Morita was nominated for an Academy Award in 1985 for *The Karate Kid*, and he received the Lifetime Achievement Award from the Association of Asian/Pacific American Artists in 1987. He also acted on *Happy Days*, an old television show.

Lawson Fusao Inada (b. 1938)

Writing can be fun. Lawson Fusao Inada (foo-sah-oh ee-nah-dah) is the co-owner of Kids Matter, a publishing company for children. His company is a place where more kids can become writers like we are.

Mr. Inada wrote the first book of poetry by an Asian-American that was published by a large company. Mr. Inada's most famous book, called *Before the War*, was published in 1971 (New York: William Morrow). He has also written books of poetry and many other books that have been published by more than ten companies.

Mr. Inada was one of 21 American writers chosen to read his poetry at the White House. He taught classes in six states about different backgrounds and ways of learning. Mr. Inada has read and spoken at major colleges all over the U.S.

In 1984, he received an award for excellence in teaching from the Oregon State Board of Higher Education. In 1985, Mr. Inada served as the U.S. representative to the World Cultural Festival in Berlin, Germany. He also lectured throughout that country. Mr. Inada is currently serving on the Commission on Racism and Bias in Education.

Daniel Nakamura (b. 1957)

Do you like to fold things? Daniel Nakumura (nah-kah-moo-rah) is the king of origami (oh-ree-gah-mee), the art of Japanese paper folding.

Mr. Nakamura is famous for his amazing creations of paper cranes, life-size penguins, and enormous roses. He learned his origami skill from his grandma.

Mr. Nakamura was born in 1957. Mr. Nakamura's family is also very artistic. His brother is a recognized illustrator and teaches at the Art Center College of Design. His uncle is the designer of some of the early Corvette automobiles.

Courtesy of *Tozai Times*

Mr. Daniel Nakamura, the king of origami

Mr. Nakamura once had to make a crane out of a piece of paper 19 feet by 18 feet. big! The paper he worked with is larger than the carpet in our bedrooms! He doesn't do only origami for a living, he also makes sculptures and paints with watercolors, and he teaches at Venice High School in California.

We did origami in our workshop, and we thought it was fun. Try it!

MORE FAMOUS FIRSTS AND HEROES

Here are some more people you may want to learn about. There is a new encyclopedia out about famous Japanese Americans. It is called *An A to Z Japanese American History: Reference from 1868 to the Present* (New York: Facts on File, 1993). This might be a good place for you to look for more stuff.

Mitsuye Endo (mee-tsoo-eh ehn-do) (b. 1920)

Won the first favorable court decision for the Nisei about the internment camps.

Warren Furutani (foo-roo-tah-nee) (b. 1947)

First Japanese American to be president of the Los Angeles city school system.

Samuel Hayakawa (hah-yah-kah-wah) (1906–1992)

Served as California state senator from 1977 to 1982.

John Kiyoshi Hirasaki (kee-yoh-shee hee-rah-sah-kee) (b. 1941)

NASA manned spacecraft scientist.

Lorie Hirose (heee-roh-seh) (b. 1961)

Won an Emmy Award in 1991 for her work on a documentary. Works as a reporter for 9-KUSA News in Denver, Colorado.

William Hosokawa (hoh-soh-kah-wah) (b. 1915)

First foreign correspondent for the *Denver Post.* Wrote *Nisei: The Quiet Americans* in 1969.

Mamoru Iga (mah-moh-roo ee-gah) (b. 1916)

Author of *The Thorn in the Chyrsanthemum: Suicide and Economic Success in Modern Japan.*

Daniel K. Inouye (ee-noh-oo-eh) (b. 1924)

First Japanese American elected to U.S. Senate (represented Hawaii). Fought in WWII and earned a Distinguished Service Cross.

Tomi Kanaazawa (toh-mee kah-nah-zah-wah)

First Nisei to appear in a leading role with the Metropolitan Opera Company.

Saburo Kido (sah-boo-roh kee-doh) (1902–1977)

Founded the Japanese American Citizens League in 1930.

Jin Kinoshita (jeen kee-nohsh-tah) (b. 1922)

An ophthalmologist who pioneered research on "sugar" cataracts.

Ann Kiyomura (kee-yoh-moo-rah) (b. 1955)

Won Wimbledon women's doubles title in 1975.

Tommy Kono (koh-noh) (b. 1930)

Won Olympic weight-lifting titles for the U.S. in 1952 and 1956, and a silver medal in 1960.

Ben Kuroki (koo-roh-kee) (b. 1918)

Won the Air Force Distinguished Flying Cross as a gunner on a bomber in WWII.

William Marutani (mah-roo-tah-nee) (b. 1923)

First Japanese American lawyer to argue and win a case before the Supreme Court.

Doris Matsui (mah-tsoo-ee) (b. 1944)

Appointed to President Clinton's cabinet as Deputy Director of Public Liaison for the President.

Robert Matsui (mah-tsoo-ee) (b. 1941)

Elected to represent California in the U.S. House of Representatives in 1979.

George Matsumoto (maht-soo-moh-toh) (b. 1922)

Recipient of numerous awards in architecture.

Shigemi Matsumoto (shee-geh-mee mah-tsoo-MOH-toh)

Rising opera singer and the only Japanese American member of the San Francisco Opera Company.

Masayuki Matsunaga (mah-sah-yoo-kee mah-tsoo-nah-gah) (1916–1990)

Served as U.S. Representative from Hawaii and was a major supporter of the redress bill.

Cynthia Mayeda (mah-eh-dah) (b. 1949)

Leader in the field of business and charitable organizations.

Hiroshi "Hershey" Miyamoto (hee-roh-shee mee-yah-moh-toh) (b. 1926)

Congressional Medal of Honor recipient.

Frank Shotaro Miyamota (shoh-tah-roh mee-yah-moh-tah) (b. 1912)

Sociologist at the University of Washington.

Kent Nagano (nah-gah-noh) (b. 1951)

International conductor currently with the Berkeley Symphony.

Isamu Noguchi (ee-sah-moo noh-goo-chee) (1904–1988)

Noted sculptor, best known for the relief sculpture he created for the Associated Press building in Rockefeller Center in New York. He was also a consultant for the design of John F. Kennedy's tomb.

Sono Osato (soh-noh oh-sah-toh) (b. 1919)

Dancer with the famous Ballet Russe.

James Sakamoto (sah-kah-moh-toh) (1903–1955)

First Nisei boxer to fight professionally at Madison Square Garden.

Makoto Sakamoto (ma-koh-toh sah-kah-moh-toh) (b. 1947)

Led the U.S. men's gymnastics squad in the Tokyo Olympics in 1964.

Eric Sato (sah-toh) (b. 1966)

Played on the 1992 U.S. Olympic men's volleyball team with his brother Gary.

Gary Sato (sah-toh) (b. 1955)

Played on the 1992 U.S. Olympic men's volleyball team with his brother Eric.

Liana Sato (sah-toh) (b. 1964)

Played on the 1992 U.S. Olympic women's volleyball team. Eric and Gary Sato are her brothers.

Kosaku Sawada (koh-sah-koo sah-wah-dah)

Developed new varieties of camellias.

Suma Sugi (soo-mah soo-gee) (b. 1906)

In 1930, became the first Nisei lobbyist.

Pat Suzuki (soo-zoo-kee) (b. 1931)

Recording star and actress. Her outstanding role was the lead in *The Flower Drum Song.*

Joseph Swensen (b. 1960)

Famous violinist and graduate of Juilliard School of Music.

Shinkichi Tajiri (sheen-kee-chee tah-jee-ree) (b. 1923)

Famous sculptor of bronze and brass. Has received many honors and awards.

Irene Takahashi (tah-kah-hah-shee)

Lawyer and municipal court judge in California.

Jokichi Takamine (joh-kee-chee tah-kah-mee-neh) (1854–1922)

A chemist, was the first to isolate pure adrenaline. He founded the Nippon Club in New York to improve understanding of U.S. and Japanese relations.

Tritia Toyota (toy-yoh-tah)

One of the first Japanese American news anchors on television. She works in the Los Angeles area.

Miyoshi Umeki (mee-yoh-shee oo-meh-kee) (b. 1929)

Won an Academy Award as Best Supporting Actress in 1957 for the movie *Sayonara.*

Newton (Uyesugi) Wesley (oo-eh-soo-gee)

An optometrist whose work played a large part in perfecting plastic contact lenses.

Rev. Seigen Haruo Yamaoka (say-gehn hah-roo-oh yah-mah-oh-kah) (b. 1934)

First Nisei to be Bishop of Buddhist Church of America in San Francisco.

Thomas Yatabe (yah-tah-beh) (b. 1897)

First Nisei licensed to practice dentistry in California. First national president of the Japanese American Citizens League.

Karl Yoneda (yoh-neh-dah) (b. 1906)

Author of *History of Japanese Labor in the United States.*

Hideki Yukawa (hee-deh-kee yoo-kah-wah) (1907–1981)

Received the Nobel Prize for Physics.

STORIES, POETRY, AND LANGUAGE

Many times we learn a lesson that will last,
From things that happened in the past.
You can learn a lot from what we have told,
Stories, language, haiku, as precious as gold.

This fun chapter tells you about all kinds of neat things about stories and wonderful books to read. It might teach you some new words in the Japanese language or inspire you to write *haiku* poems. Read on and learn more about Japanese American stories, poetry, and language.

FOLK TALES

Cranes, kites, dragons, magic talking animals, and princesses—these are all things you can find in *mukashi banashi* (mookah-shee bah-nah-shee), Japanese folk tales. Japanese tales are important because they teach valuable lessons. Some of these lessons include being respectful, kind, or helpful and always doing your best.

Children learn Japanese tales in many dif-ferent ways. They learn them from books, from songs, or at school. During World War II, Japanese American parents and grandparents in the internment camps told the tales aloud to children. Through the generations as the tales were told and retold, people changed them. So there might be more than a hundred ways to tell just one story.

Chris Tucker

Young authors and teachers enjoying stories

We have found there are some common features in most Japanese tales. Older people are often the good people in the story because older people are highly respected in Japanese culture. Not every tale has a happy ending, which is is very different from most American and European fairy tales. The two folk tales we have included here do have happy endings. They are about animals, jokes, and ordinary people, places, and things.

There are more than 15,000 Japanese folk tales and legends that have been written down, which is more than any country in the Western part of the world. Many of them have been told by more than one author. Sometimes one folk tale is retold by several authors in different books. In our book we only have room to retell two folk tales. If you like these, you can always go to the library and find more. Here are three tales we read. We hope you like them as much as we did.

Momotaro, the Peach Boy

This folk tale is known by most Japanese American kids. They hear it from their grandparents or parents. Some read it in books of folk tales. Others may learn it from the song "Momotaro" (moh-moh-tah-roh). This is a popular folk tale in Japan, too. We learned it by reading the book Momotaro, The Peach Boy, *retold and illustrated by Linda Shute (New York: Lathrop, Lee, and Shepard Books, 1986).*

Once upon a time in old Japan there lived an old couple who prayed for a child to take care of them in their old age. One day, the old woman was washing clothes in the river when she saw a gigantic peach floating in the river. She reached out and lifted the peach into her laundry basket to take home for dinner.

"Boy, am I hungry," her husband announced when he came home from cutting wood. He wanted to cut the peach the instant his wife showed it to him. All of a sudden a voice came from the peach, saying, "Don't cut! Don't cut!"

"Gracious!" said the old woman.

The peach split open and a baby boy popped out. The old man and woman said, "You were brought from heaven to answer our prayers. We will call you Momotaro, which means 'peach boy.'"

The parents gave him love and care. With every meal he got stronger and bigger. When Momotaro was full grown he decided to go to the island of the oni (OH-nee), who were vicious and greedy crea-

tures that stole from others. His parents sadly gave him their blessings.

The next day he set off on his journey with his sword, a banner with his peach emblem on it, an iron war fan, and three *kibi dango* (kee-bee dahn-goh), which are rice dumplings. He sat down to eat one of his kibi dango when a skinny dog came along and said, "I am starving!"

Momotaro felt sorry for the dog and said, "I can do without one kibi dango." So he gave one to the hungry dog.

The grateful dog decided to help Momotaro fight his battle with the oni. Soon they saw a hungry monkey and a pheasant. Momotaro gave them his last two kibi dango. The delicious kibi dango made them stronger, and they too decided to join Momotaro.

The four friends went over the mountain and reached the ocean. They got onto a boat and headed toward the island of the oni. When they got there, Momotaro told the pheasant to fly above the wall and spy on the oni. The monkey climbed over the wall and unlocked the gate. Momotaro sneaked up on the oni. He yelled, "We are here to get the stolen goods back for our village people."

"You must be kidding. We are not afraid of you," yelled the vicious oni king.

The battle against the oni began. The dog bit at their ankles, the monkey pulled their ears, the pheasant pecked at their eyes and heads, and Momotaro used his sword to fight the oni. The oni were so confused that they thought they were fighting a large army. The oni king surrendered and gave back the stolen treasures.

Momotaro and his friends brought the treasures back to their villagers. At Momotaro's home, they had the best kibi dango in all of Japan, and they all lived happily ever after.

Three Strong Women

We learned this tale from reading the book Three Strong Women: A Tall Tale from Japan, *by Claus Stamm, illustrated by Jean and Mou-sien Tseng (New York: Viking Penguin, 1990).*

There once was a wrestler named Forever Mountain who thought he was very strong. On his way to the emperor's wrestling match, he saw a girl named Marume (mah-

and large bundles of wood. He wrestled with the grandmother each night. Finally, after three months of training, he could hold the old woman down for only thirty seconds! He had grown very fond of the family, and asked Marume to marry him when he returned from the wrestling match.

At the competition, Forever Mountain beat the first man just by stamping his foot. Everyone was scared. No one would go against him, so he won the prize money. The emperor made him promise not to wrestle anymore because he was so much stronger than the rest. Forever Mountain returned and became a farmer and married Marume. They all lived happily ever after.

How the Withered Trees Blossomed

We learned this story from a book made the way books in Japan are made. It opens on the left, rather than on the right like books do in our country. Each page of this book includes an illustration and the story in both English and Japanese Hiragana *(hee-rah-gah-nah) characters. Japanese writing starts on the right and goes left, instead of left to right, like ours, and it is written from the top to the bottom of the page. This book is by Miyoko Matsutani and illustrated by Yasuo Segawa (Philadelphia: Lippincott, 1969).*

A long time ago, there was a kind old couple living in the country. One day, the old man went fishing and put his fishing basket in the river. His mean neighbor saw the

roo-meh) carrying a bucket of water on her head. He wanted to make her laugh and drop the bucket so he could fill it up for her and show off his strength. When Forever Mountain tickled Marume, she trapped his hand underneath her arm. Forever Mountain was sure he could get away, but he was stuck.

"You're hurting my hand. Please let go!" he begged.

Marume said, "I'll let you go if you come to my house. My grandmother, my mom, and I will help you get stronger for the wrestling match. Our amazing strength will surprise you."

Forever Mountain followed Marume to her home. There, he trained by doing the work of many men, carrying heavy loads such as cows, gigantic buckets of water,

kind old man and put his own fishing basket upstream so that he would catch all the fish before they swam into the kind old man's basket.

The next day, the mean neighbor went to see if he had caught any fish, but all he had in his basket was a thick old root. He said in an angry voice, "All I caught was a crummy root!" The mean neighbor then went to the kind old man's basket and saw that he had a basket full of fish. He stole the fish and put his old root into the old man's basket.

When the old man went to check his basket and saw the old root, he said, "At least I caught something. I can use this root for firewood." He took the root home to split and dry it. But when he split the root, a cute little white puppy jumped out of it! The old couple named the puppy Shiro (shee-roh), which means "white."

They fed Shiro and loved him, and he grew bigger and bigger. One day, Shiro really surprised the old couple when he started talking. He said, "Put a saddle and straw bag on me and bring a spade, then hop onto my back." The old man said, "Oh no, I can't do that! I'm too heavy for you and I will break your back!" But Shiro answered, "No, you won't. Just do what I say." So the old man did.

Shiro took the old man up into the mountains and told him to dig in a special spot. The old man did as the dog told him to do.

While the old man was digging, his spade hit precious gems and gold that were buried there. He put them in the straw bags and took them home to show his wife. They emptied the bags into big piles of gold and jewels and joyfully played with them. The mean neighbor heard the "clink, clink, clink" of the gold and ran over to see where the kind man had found the treasure.

After the kind man told him how he got the gold, the mean neighbor asked to borrow Shiro. The mean man and his wife beat Shiro and forced him to show them where to dig. When the old man started digging, all he found were snakes, worms, and dirt. "You made us feel ridiculous!" yelled the mean old man. He beat Shiro with the spade and killed him.

The mean couple buried Shiro in the mountains and planted a willow tree in the spot. They went back to the kind old couple's house and told them what had happened. The kind old couple sobbed and missed Shiro very much.

The next day, the kind old man went up into the mountains to visit the spot where the dog was buried and saw that the willow tree had grown. The old man cut off a branch to take home to remember Shiro.

At home, he carved a bowl out of the wood. When the old couple ground rice in the bowl, the rice turned into gold. The mean old woman came over to see what all the racket was about. After they told her what had happened, she borrowed the bowl. When she took the bowl home and ground her rice in it, all she got was yucky, stinky dirt. She was so mad that she burned the bowl and returned the ashes to the kind neighbors. The neighbors were very sad because the bowl was a treasure to them to remember Shiro.

The kind old man decided to spread the ashes on the crab apple trees in his yard, and the trees magically bloomed with beautiful pink blossoms. His yard was gorgeous!

A prince rode by and saw the beautiful yard. "I will reward you for making the withered trees blossom," he said. "Those crab apple trees are so pretty!"

Then the mean neighbor grabbed the ashes from the old man and said, "I am the man who can make the trees more beautiful." But when he threw the ashes, they went right into the prince's eyes. The prince got so mad that he told his guards to beat the mean neighbor. The mean neighbor had to run for his life and leave his home.

The kind old couple bought some new white puppies to remind them of Shiro, and they all lived happily ever after.

BOOKS

Books are lots of fun because they teach us many things we didn't know or help us to

enjoy a story in a new way. We read many books of stories written by Japanese American authors. In this section, we tell some of our very favorite stories in our own words.

Baseball Saved Us

This is the story of how a Japanese American boy's love for baseball helped him survive the terrible time he spent in an internment camp. (See the history chapter for an explanation of internment camps.) This book is by Ken Mochizuki and illustrated by Dom Lee (New York: Lee and Low, 1993).

In the camps, it was hot and dusty in the summer, and cold and windy in the winter.

The guards had guns and watched the people all the time. People in the camps became sad, bored, and angry.

One boy's father decided to make a baseball field to help people forget about their sadness and anger. The grown-ups and the kids all helped pull up the sagebrush to clear the field near the barracks where they lived. The guard in the tower watched them work every day.

Soon the field was ready, and the baseball games began, with grown-ups and kids playing together. All summer, the Japanese Americans played baseball, which became a big event in the camp. The whole time, the guard continued to watch. The boy whose father decided to make the baseball field was not a very good player and everyone always made fun of him. But he never gave up.

During the last game of the season, his team was in the championships, and they were losing by one point. The boy came up to bat. He heard the other team hollering, "Easy out!" As the other team teased him, the boy looked up and saw the

sun glinting off the guard's sunglasses. The boy was so sick of being watched by guards all the time that he got angry and really whacked the ball with all his might. His home run won the game and everyone cheered for him! Even the guard in the tower smiled and gave him a thumbs-up sign.

You may think this is a happy ending to the story, but remember the Japanese Americans were still held in the camp. Finally, the Japanese Americans were allowed to go, and the boy returned to his old school. It was bad before he went to camp, but now it was even worse. Children called him rotten mean names like "Jap."

Later in the year, the boy joined a baseball team at his school. The kids at school thought he was an "easy out" too. One day at a game, the crowd was shouting, "The Jap's no good!" As the boy stepped up to bat, he looked over at the pitcher and saw the sun glint off his glasses and remembered the guard in the tower. The boy got really angry again and swung the bat with all his might. He hit the ball and watched it sail over the fence once again.

Crow Boy

This story is about a boy who was made fun of because he did things differently from the way others did them. Some people didn't want to read this book because it has a picture of a person on the front that isn't drawn very well. This book taught us an important lesson, the one teachers always say: "Never judge a book by its

cover." We decided to give the book a try. We really liked this book and hope you do, too. If you do judge a book by its cover, you might miss out on something wonderful that is inside. This book is by Taro Yashima (New York: Viking Press, 1983).

Once there was a little boy in Japan called Chibi (chee-bee), which means "little boy." Chibi was not well liked at his school. He was always left alone to eat and to play, and he stood at the end of every line. Chibi didn't try to make any friends, and he pretended not to listen to his teachers. He picked up gross bugs that no one else would even look at, and everyone thought he was strange. His classmates and the grown-ups called him stupid and slow-poke. Chibi learned how to cross his eyes so that he wouldn't have to see the mean and ugly faces other kids made at him.

Finally, Chibi got a nice sixth grade teacher, Mr. Isobe (ee-soh-beh), who really liked him a lot. Mr. Isobe took the class on many field trips. Chibi knew a lot about the flowers in the garden, and he knew where wild grapes and potatoes grew. This made Mr. Isobe very happy. Mr. Isobe even talked with Chibi when nobody was around.

One day, Chibi's school had a talent show. When Chibi stood on the stage, everyone said, "Why is Chibi up there?" and, "He is too stupid to do anything."

Mr. Isobe told the audience that Chibi would make the voices of crows. First, Chibi made the voice of a newly hatched crow. Next he made the voices of mother and father crows. Finally he made the sound of the crows that lived near his home. The sounds he made were so lonely that they made everyone sad. When Chibi was done, the audience clapped and had tears in their eyes because they remembered how badly they had treated Chibi. Mr. Isobe told everyone how far Chibi had to walk to school every day and that while he walked, Chibi listened to the crow calls.

After that, everyone felt differently about Chibi. They understood him better. On graduation day, Chibi was the only student with perfect attendance for all six years. From that day on, no one called him Chibi, they called him Crow Boy. He really liked his new name and whenever he walked, he would make the voice of a happy crow.

OTHER GOOD BOOKS

Here are a few suggestions for more Japanese and Japanese American stories and folk tales we liked. Read them and you might like them, too!

A to Zen, by Ruth Wells, illustrated by Yoshi (Saxonville: Picture Book Studio, 1992). Using the letters of the English alphabet, *A to Zen* describes 26 Japanese words. This book opens like a traditional Japanese book, on the left, which is the opposite way Western books are opened.

The Badger and the Magic Fan, by Tony Johnston, illustrated by Tomie dePaola (New York: Putnam, 1990). This book is about a mean badger who tricks the *tengu* (tehn-goo), or goblin children, into giving him a magic fan. By the end of the book, the badger ends up wishing he had never played the trick.

Faithful Elephants, by Yukio Tsuchiya, illustrated by Ted Lewin (Boston: Houghton Mifflin, 1988). This is a true story of three elephants in the Tokyo zoo that were killed because the zookeepers were afraid all the dangerous animals would run wild through the city during the war.

Mouse's Marriage, written and illustrated by Junko Morimoto (New York: Viking Penguin, 1986). A mouse is looking for a husband who is the mightiest in the world. Her search is long and tiring, but she finally finds the best husband.

A Pair of Red Clogs, written by Masako Matsuno, illustrated by Kazue Mizumura (New York: The World Publishing Co., 1960). A girl gets a brand new pair of red clogs. When one clog gets cracked while she plays a game, she tries to trick her mother into getting her a new pair.

The Paper Crane, by Molly Bang (New York: Greenwillow Books, 1985). A poor restaurant owner gets a magic paper crane that comes to life and dances for his customers.

The Rooster Who Understood Japanese, by Yoshiko Uchida, illustrated by Charles Robinson (New York: Charles Scribner's Sons, 1976). This is a story of an old woman who has many pets, including a

rooster named Mr. Lincoln who under-
stands Japanese.

Sachiko Means Happiness, by Kimiko
Sakai, illustrated by Tomie Arai (San Fran-
sisco: Children's Book Press, 1990). This
story is about a girl named Sachiko (sah-
chee-koh), which means "happiness." Her
grandmother has Alzheimer's disease and
thinks she is a little girl again.

Sadako and the Thousand Paper Cranes,
written by Eleanor Coerr, paintings by
Ronald Himler (New York: Dell Publishing,
1977). There are many books about the
atom bomb that was dropped on
Hiroshima, Japan, during World War II. This
book is probably the most well-known of
them. It is the true story of a real girl who
was affected by the bomb.

The Stonecutter, written and illustrated
by Gerald McDermott (New York: Penguin,
1978). Tasaku (Tah-sah-koo) wishes to
become many things, but he discovers his
own foolishness.

Tree of Cranes, written and illustrated by
Allen Say (Boston: Houghton Mifflin, 1991).

A young boy in Japan learns the story of an
important American holiday. The book also
has very beautiful illustrations.

More books are coming out all the time,
so ask your librarians about good books
about heritage. P.S. Remember to tell them
about this book written by kids, too!

HAIKU

Haiku (hy-koo) is a form of poetry that is
about three hundred years old. Each haiku
has 17 syllables in all. A syllable is the smallest part of a word and is counted by how
many times your chin goes down when you
say the word. The first and third lines of a
haiku have five syllables, and the second
line has seven.

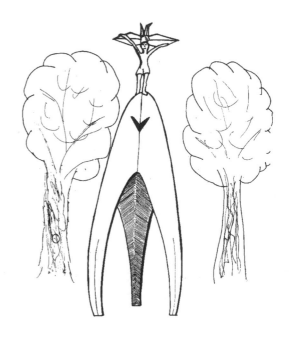

Haiku poets write about seasons and nature, but you can write about anything you like. Whatever you choose to write about, your haiku should make readers see what you're writing about in a new and different way. Remember, haikus don't have to rhyme.

Here is an easy way to get started on your haiku:

1. Pick a topic to write about.
2. Write as many five and seven syllable lines about your topic as you can think of.
3. Choose your favorite five-syllable line for the first line of your haiku.
4. Choose your favorite seven-syllable line for the second line.
5. Choose another five-syllable line for the third line.

You have just written your own haiku! Here are some we wrote:

Big, bright, full colors
soaring up into the wind,
kites fly high and proud.

Festive, happy, hot,
dancing, eating together
on a July night.

The wind is screaming.
It makes the trees blow crazy,
makes them fall apart.
Elegant seagull
flies through the air gracefully
far above the clouds.

Water is dripping,
a puddle of water on
the pretty flowers.

LANGUAGE

We learned a lot about the Japanese language. We learned about the different ways to write Japanese. We'll teach you some words and expressions in Japanese, and even the Japanese names and sounds of certain animals..

Japanese Language School

Many Nisei, Sansei, and Yonsei went to *Nihongakko* (nee-hohn-GAH-koh), or Japanese language school, when they were kids. Some went on Saturdays, some on Sundays, and some even went after their regular school during the week. The classes were held at Buddhist temples, community centers, and Japanese American churches.

At Nihongakko, children learned Japanese words, origami, songs, folk tales, and how to write Japanese characters. Some Nihongakko even had recitals, so the children could show their parents what they had learned.

Parents wanted their children to attend Nihongakko because they wanted their kids to learn about their Japanese heritage. Some of the children didn't like the idea, but they did like meeting new Japanese American friends. Today, many Sansei and Yonsei parents still send their children to Nihongakko.

Writing Japanese

Did you know that there are three ways to write in Japanese? They are *kanji* (kan-gee), *hiragana* (hee-rah-gah-nah), and *katakana* (kah-tah-kah-nah).

Kanji is used for formal writing and signs. Kanji characters were adapted from Chinese characters. It is the hardest way of writing to learn. Each kanji character is a stick-figure picture of what it represents. A kanji character sometimes stands for a whole word. Only about 2,000 kanji are used regularly, but there are over 45,000 in a complete dictionary. Here are examples of some kanji characters:

This is *ki* (kee), the word for "tree." Can you see the roots of the tree in this word?

When you put lots of trees together, you get the word *mori* (moh-ree), which means "forest." Can you see all the trees in the forest?

This is *hito* (hee-toh), the Kanji word for "person." Can you see the body and legs of a walking person?

The second style of writing is Hiragana. It is used more in everyday life and is easier to write than kanji. Hiragana is like an alphabet, because to create a word from it, you need more than one character.

The last form is katakana. This is used for the words that were not originally used by the Japanese. Such words could be foreign words brought to Japan, such as "hamburger," or someone's name in English, French, or another language.

It is not very hard to pronounce Japanese words. The five vowels are always pronounced the same way, like this:

a = "ah" as in "father"
i = "ee" as in "machine"
u = "oo" as in "tooth"
e = "eh" as in "get"
o = "oh" as in "hope"

Counting In Japanese

We all know how to count from one to ten, but do you know how to count in Japanese? There are several ways. Here's one:

one = *ichi* (ee-chee)
two = *ni* (nee)
thrcc = *san* (sahn)
four = *shi* (shee)
five = *go* (goh)
six = *roku* (ro-koo)
seven = *shichi* (shee-chee)
eight = *hachi* (hah-chee)
nine = *ku* (koo)
ten = *ju* (joo)

Animals and Their Sounds

Have you ever wondered what animals are called in Japanese? Did you know that in Japanese dogs don't say "bow-wow," they say "wan-wan"? We thought you might be interested to learn the names and sounds of animals in Japanese. See the box below.

ENGLISH		JAPANESE	
Animal	**Sound**	**Animal**	**Sound**
dog	bow-wow	*inu* (ee-noo)	*wan-wan* (wahn-wahn)
cat	meow	*neko* (neh-koh)	*nya* (nyah)
frog	ribbet	*kaeru* (kah-eh-roo)	*kero-kero* (keh-roh keh-roh)
cow	moo	*ushi* (oo-shee)	*mo* (moh)
pig	oink	*buta* (boo-tah)	*bu* (boo)
sheep	baa	*hitsuji* (hee-tsoo-jee)	*me* (meh)
rooster	cock-a-doodle-doo	*ondori* (ohn-doh-ree)	*koke kokko* (koh-keh kohk-koh)
bird	cheep cheep	*tori* (toh-ree)	*chi chi* (chee-chee)
mouse	squeak	*nezumi* (neh-zoo-mee)	*chu chu* (choo-choo)
duck	quack	*ahiru* (ah-hee-roo)	*kuwa kuwa* (koo-wah, koo-wah)

you're welcome – *do itashimashite* (doh ee-tah-shee-mahsh-teh)

I'm sorry – *gomen nasai* (goh-mehn nah-sigh)

how are you? – *genki desu ka* (gehn-kee dehs-ka)

I'm fine – *genki des* (gehn-kee dehs)

I'm sad – *kanashi* (kah-nah-shee)

I'm happy – *ureshi* (oo-reh-shee)

tough it out – *gaman* (gah-mahn)

let's go – *ikimasho* (ee-kee-mah-shoh)

Expressions and Salutations

These are words you will want to know if you want to speak Japanese. In fact, many Japanese Americans use these expressions and salutations here in America. (A salutation is a greeting, like "good morning," or a polite expression, like "thank you.")

good morning – *ohayo gozaimasu* (oh-hah-yo goh-zah-ee-mahs)

good day – *konnichi wa* (kohn-nee-chee wah)

good evening – *konban wa* (kohn-bahn wah)

good night – *oyasumi nasai* (o-yah-soo-mee nah-sigh)

good-bye – *sayonara* (sah-yoh-nah-rah)

thank you – *domo arigato gozaimasu* (doh-moh ah-ree-gah-toh goh-zah-ee-mahs)

Common Japanese Words

Did you know that Americans use some Japanese words in our TV commercials, in restaurants, in stores, and in some of the phrases we say? Here are a few examples:

- We've seen different *dojos* (doh-johs), or martial arts schools, around the city that teach *karate* (kah-rah-teh), *judo* (joo-doh), and *kendo* (kehn-doh).
- Some stores sell *zoris* (zoh-rees), or thongs, every summer. Some stores also sell beautiful *kimonos* (kee-mohn-nohs), or long robes.
- Students call their teachers *sensei* (sehn-say) in the dojos, just like they did in the *Karate Kid* and Teenage Mutant Ninja Turtle movies.
- We've heard people say, *"Sayonara"* (sah-yoh-nah-rah) to each other to say "good-bye."

- People say, "I'll have *s'kosh*" (s'kohsh) if they want only "a little bit" of something.
- A few bedding and furniture stores here sell *futon* (foo-tohn) beds.
- *Sushi* (soo-shee), *tempura* (tehm-poo-rah), and *teriyaki* (teh-ree-yah-kee) are the names of some of the foods served in Japanese restaurants.
- Nowadays, *karaoke* (kah-rah-oh-keh) singing is popular in nightclubs, restaurants, and at parties. Karaoke singers get up on stage and sing along to a taped song.

The next time you hear or see these words, you can say that you know they come from the Japanese language.

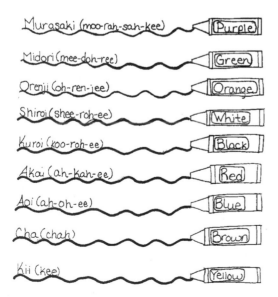

Murasaki (moo-rah-sah-kee) — Purple
Midori (mee-doh-ree) — Green
Orenji (oh-ren-jee) — Orange
Shiroi (shee-roh-ee) — White
Kuroi (koo-roh-ee) — Black
Akai (ah-kah-ee) — Red
Aoi (ah-oh-ee) — Blue
Cha (chah) — Brown
Kii (kee) — Yellow

Borrowed Words

Some English words have made it into the Japanese language, just like we have brought some some Japanese words into English. Here are a few examples:

baseball – *beisuboru* (bay-soo-boh-roo)
Batman – *Battoman* (baht-oh-mahn)

boss – *bosu* (boh-soo)
Coca Cola – *Koka Koura* (koh-ka koh-rah)
coffee – *kohi* (koh-hee)
hamburger – *hanbaga* (hahn-bah-gah)
hot dog – *hotto doggu* (hoht-oh doh-goo)
McDonalds – *Makudonarudo* (mah-koo-
    doh-nah-roo-doh)
orange – *orenji* (oh-rehn-jee)
Pepsi – *Pepushi* (peh-poo-shee)
pizza – *piza* (pee-zah)
rocket – *roketto* (ro-keht-oh)
salad – *sarada* (sah-rah-dah)
spaghetti – *supaggeti* (soo-pah-geh-tee)
Walkman – *Wokuman* (woh-koo-mahn)

Chris Tucker

The young authors interviewing the storyteller

We hope you have enjoyed learning about stories, poetry and language. Remember, there are many more books at the library for you to read on these subjects.

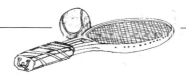

REAL PEOPLE

People are wonderful, people are great,
Happy stories, sad stories, they're all first rate.
We all learn from the stories of another,
Remember, they are someone's sister or brother.

Japanese Americans are very proud of their heritage. Their traditions are as fascinating as the stories of their lives. We learned a lot from interviewing Japanese Americans and writing about them. Following a dream was common to all the people we talked to. We also learned that Japanese Americans value education and family. Even though these Japanese Americans followed different dreams, they are the same in many ways. They showed us their perseverance, determination, and faith.

In this section, you will read real-life stories about professors, athletes, ministers, businesspeople, and others of all ages. We felt very honored that our "real people" were willing to share their stories with us. Many of them told us it is hard to talk about themselves, because it is not part of the Japanese American culture to tell about yourself. This makes these stories even more special.

George Inai

If you walk into the Pacific Mercantile store in Sakura Square in Denver, Colorado, you will see Mr. George Inai (ee-nye) sitting in his chair near the back of the store. Mr. Inai is one hundred years old. He goes to his store every day. In the store, you will find four generations of his family. His daughter and granddaughter help run the store, and his great-granddaughter plays because she is too little to work.

When we met Mr. Inai, we walked around his store and saw bean sauce, hot peppers, pickled ginger, octopus, sushi, and anchovies. We also saw tea cups, rice bowls, rice cookers, and *hashi* (chop-

Chris Tucker

Mr. George Inai

cery store. That one store then grew into a chain of three stores.

On April 8, 1925, Mr. Inai married Takako Takeuchi (tah-kah-koh tah-keh-oo-chee). They had four children. When World War II began, something awful happened to Mr. Inai and his family. Mr. Inai had to sell his stores because the American government was relocating most Japanese American citizens. His family packed their clothes and blankets and whatever they could carry. They had to leave many of their valuable things behind, and other Americans took and used them for their own homes. Mr. Inai and his family were moved to an internment camp in Tule Lake, California. Later, they were moved to a camp in Topaz, Utah. While they were at the internment camps,

sticks). The rice candy is best, because you can eat the inside wrapping paper and it tastes good.

Mr. Inai has had an interesting life. He was born on January 5, 1893, in Japan. In 1915 he came to the United States. When he got to America, he changed his name from Yutaka (yoo-tah-kah) to George so he could fit into the American way of life.

For a while, Mr. Inai lived with his brother and worked in an orchard near San Francisco. After experiencing hard times because their crops failed, Mr. Inai decided to move to Sacramento, where he worked at a grocery store as a delivery man. Then he worked for the American Poultry company as a bookkeeper. Mr. Inai just kept working at all kinds of jobs until he was able to save enough money to buy a gro-

Chris Tucker

Mr. George Inai with his great-granddaughter

the Japanese Americans had to sleep on straw mattresses on the floor.

Toward the end of the war, Mr. Inai was given permission to leave the camp so he could start a grocery store in Denver along with his friend, Mr. George Oyama (oh-yah-mah). They wanted to name the store "Japan Mercantile." But because it was still wartime, the Denver City Council recommended they choose a different name. Mr. Inai chose "Pacific Mercantile." He named his store after the ocean he sailed across when he came to the United States.

But even a successful business could not save Mr. Inai from sadness. After 46 years of marriage, his wife died.

In 1974, three years after Mrs. Inai died, Mr. Inai was awarded the Fourth Order Merit by the Emperor of Japan for the community work he performed in the United States. One of the important jobs he worked on was to get a bronze bust in memory of Governor Ralph Carr. Governor Carr welcomed Japanese Americans to the state of Colorado during World War II while the rest of America seemed to be trying to get rid of them.

In 1993, after four children, 13 grandchildren, and two great-grandchildren, Mr. Inai celebrated his 100th birthday.

Mr. Inai is a very lucky man to live so long. We hope that many more people will be able to live as long as Mr. Inai so others can learn from their experiences.

Sue Yamamoto Ando

Business was booming! "Japanese American Woman Successful Hog Raiser" flashed the headlines from not only local but also international newspapers. The articles were about Sue Yamamoto Ando (yah-mah-moh-toh ahn-doh) and her special achievements. In the early 1900s, there weren't many successful businesswomen, let alone Japanese American businesswomen.

Sue Yamamoto Ando was born in Utah on August 27, 1906. She was the only child born to her mother and father. When she was seven, her parents started a hog ranch. Her father had a heart problem and died when she was nine. Her mother, who was a very strong woman, decided to keep working as a hog rancher and moved the farm to San Bernardino, California. To help out, Mrs. Ando would come home after school and get big buckets of water to fill the hogs' water troughs.

Mrs. Sue Yamamoto Ando

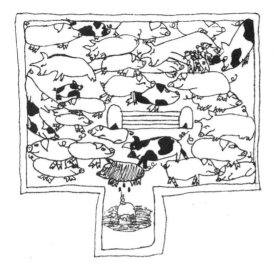

Since she had to work so hard, Mrs. Ando had a very lonely life with little time for friends. The hog ranch had three hundred to four hundred hogs at that time. After she completed high school, she took over the ranch because her mother couldn't handle it anymore. Although Mrs. Ando had dreams of being a doctor, she felt that taking over the ranch and helping her mother was the right thing to do.

On July 10, 1929, she married John S. Ando. He was attending law school when they got married. There was so much work on the ranch, he quit school to help his wife. Mrs. Ando moved many of the hogs to Long Beach, California. She continued to run the San Bernardino ranch as well. Mrs. Ando was so successful that she was able to bid for a garbage contract to get more land and to get 25 to 30 tons of garbage each day for the hogs to eat. She won! She bought all the hogs she could get and ended up owning 6,000 hogs of her own. She kept other people's hogs on contract, too, so all together there were about 14,000 hogs.

However, soon the ranch was forced to close down because of World War II. Mrs. Ando lost both ranches when she was taken to an internment camp. The land was taken over by people who divided up the ranch. They thought the hogs and the ranch would not be useful to them.

Mrs. Ando has led a very hard-working life, a life to be respected. She appreciated her mother for teaching her to be honest and has always felt that her parents were the most important people in her life. Mrs. Ando is a Nisei. She has worked hard to be treated like other Americans. When she went to Japan, she found she wasn't accepted there either, because she had not been born there. People were very racist against her.

Mrs. Ando thinks that Dr. Martin Luther King, Jr., has helped to make all people better appreciate each other's heritage. She also feels that the contributions made by Japanese Americans who served in the 100th Battalion and 442nd Regimental Combat Team during World War II helped others see that they were loyal Americans.

Mrs. Ando is now 87 years old. She has two children, six grandchildren and five great-grandchildren. She is a widow and lives with her daughter in Placentia, California.

Mrs. Ando told us she is 100 percent American. Her advice to people is, "Be a good American, but don't forget your heritage."

George T. Sakato

Mr. George T. Sakato (sah-kah-toh) volunteered to fight for America. His rifle infantry unit had nine thousand Japanese Americans from all over the U.S. While Mr. Sakato and the other men were fighting for their country, their families were in internment camps.

His basic training was in the marshes and on the sandy beaches of Camp Blanding, Florida. He said it rained a lot, it was always hot and muggy, and they had to sleep in the forest with snakes. Mr. Sakato was not very good with a rifle, so as soon as he was overseas he got a machine gun.

Mr. Sakato told us about his friends in basic training and his long trip across the Atlantic Ocean. It took 28 days to reach Africa and then Italy. He said his bunk on the ship was a "smelly, dark hole." The bunks were like hammocks, four high and six across. Everyone on the ship was seasick. Once when Mr. Sakato was on guard duty, the ocean was so rough that he had to tie himself to a pole so he would not be washed overboard.

Finally they reached their destination near Switzerland's border. They had to march to the line of duty. The hills got steeper, and Mr. Sakato could hear machine guns firing and shells landing one mile away. While they rested, the men talked about what they would do after the war. The next thing they knew, they were being shot at. The shelling knocked Mr. Sakato 10 feet away. He was bruised and bleeding, but several of his friends were killed. This was his first experience with death.

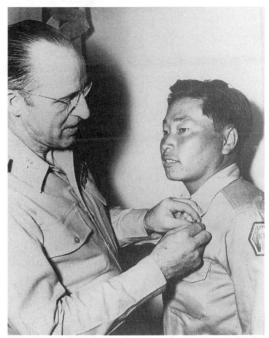

Mr. George T. Sakato receiving the Distinguished Service Cross

As they moved, the soldiers had to search for mine fields. Mr. Sakato would lie on his stomach and move about six inches while poking his bayonet into the ground to find the mines. This was very slow. If one man made a wrong move, the mine would blow up in his face. Several men's legs were blown off.

The men dug foxholes for shelter. Mr. Sakato said he was so scared when bullets whizzed over his head that he tried to crawl into his helmet, but he got better at digging foxholes! In one battle, Mr. Sakato's friends on his right and his left were hit by snipers. When the day ended, three of his friends were dead.

The platoon usually moved at night. The soliders couldn't see anything in front of them so each man held onto the back-

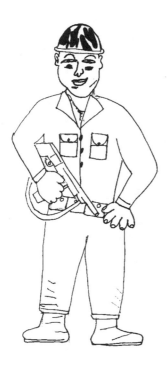

pack of the man in front of him. One dark night Mr. Sakato was leading the men. He stopped too quickly and caused a chain reaction: each man bumped into the one in front of him.

In one battle, Mr. Sakato heard gunfire and yelled at his friend Saburo (sah-boo-roh) to get down. Saburo stood up anyway and was shot. Mr. Sakato couldn't stop the bleeding and his friend died in his arms. Mr. Sakato was so angry that he jumped up and ran up the hill. He yelled to the men, "Come on! We've got to take the hill!"—and they did. Mr. Sakato later found a silver dollar that Saburo always carried with him. It was made in 1921, the year that Saburo and Mr. Sakato were born. He took it home with him and had Saburo's name engraved on it so he could always remember his friend.

There were many other battles. As the soldiers moved through the cold, wet mud, their feet turned pink and blue, and then swelled up. Mr. Sakato's feet were so cold he took off his wet socks and put them under his armpits to warm them up. Then he had to put the socks back on, even if they were still wet. He had to shove his swollen feet into his boots. The men would jokingly tell their sergeant that they needed to go home because their feet were rotting off.

One day Mr. Sakato told his commanding officer he needed to go to the aid station because he was hurt. The commanding officer saw the bullet hole in Mr. Sakato's jacket and sent him to the aid station. At the hospital, Mr. Sakato learned that he had shrapnel in his arm and chest. The doctors left the piece of metal in his chest. They told him his body would form skin around it and it would not move. He had to work hard to regain the movement of his arm.

Mr. Sakato was awarded the Distinguished Service Cross for his actions with the 442nd Regimental Combat Team while he was in the hospital. He did not even know about his award until his brother told him at the hospital. Mr. Sakato now attends all of the reunions of World War II veterans. He is proud to have fought for his country and proud to be an American.

Toshiko Kishimoto D'Elia

Toshiko (toh-shee-koh) Kishimoto (kee-shee-moh-toh) D'Elia (dah-lee-ah) became an American citizen in March of 1957. This ceremony was a very meaningful and emotional experience for her. She cried because it meant so much to her to be free after living under a military dictatorship when she was young.

Mrs. D'Elia was born in Kyoto (kyoh-toh), Japan, on January 2, 1930. She lived with her parents, her three older brothers, and one older sister. As a child, Mrs. D'Elia enjoyed going on family outings at their favorite resort and just being with her family.

Mrs. D'Elia came to the U.S. because she got a Fulbright Scholarship, and could not find a program in Japan to train for teaching children who are deaf. While Mrs. D'Elia was in America she met a man and got married without her parents' permission. After a while, she realized that her husband was not the right man for her. He loved her because she was a Japanese woman. He did not love her for the person she was inside. By that time Mrs. D'Elia was already pregnant with Erica. After her daughter was born Mrs. D'Elia decided to go back to Japan with Erica. When she got to Japan, her parents were very angry at her for not getting permission to get married and for having a baby with a man of a different culture. Mrs. D'Elia's parents said she would have to give up the baby or she was no longer welcome at their home.

Toshiko Kishimoto D'Elia was very confused. She had to choose between her family and Erica. Did she want to put Erica up for adoption and stay with her family or keep Erica and go to America? She decided to go back to America with Erica.

In America, she worked for the New York School for the Deaf and helped deaf students learn to communicate with others.

Mrs. Toshiko Kishimoto D'Elia running a marathon

One evening at a dinner party she met a pianist, Manfred D'Elia. Manfred D'Elia and Toshiko Kishimoto spent much time together. Finally they married and moved to their new home in New Jersey.

One time Mr. and Mrs. D'Elia tried to climb Mt. Rainier with friends. Mrs. D'Elia had to quit because she kept falling down, struggling, and couldn't catch her breath. The group all agreed that Mrs. D'Elia should not go further. She was frustrated that she couldn't climb the mountain, but instead of choosing to quit, she decided to get in shape. Her friend told her to run a mile every day to increase her stamina, but she wanted to accomplish more. She wanted to be the best at whatever sport she participated in.

Mrs. D'Elia with her daughter after finishing a marathon

One day, Mrs. D'Elia found a jogging book in her daughter's gym bag. This is when Erica began to coach her mom and push her to be a runner. She worked with her mom on running drills to get her in shape.

Mrs. D'Elia ran the first 26-mile marathon in New York City in 1976. Then in 1979 she became the oldest woman in the Boston Marathon to finish in less than three hours.

One day she got some bad news. The doctors told her that she had cancer and had to have an operation. Mrs. D'Elia had to quit running, and she thought she might die. At that time she was reminded of one of her students named Cheryl who stood out from the others. Cheryl had visual and hearing handicaps and had cerebral palsy. Mrs. D'Elia felt inspired when she saw all the problems Cheryl had and how she had overcome them by teaching herself to walk. She decided if Cheryl could do it then so could she. So Mrs. D'Elia began training again and in the spring of 1980 she ran again in the Boston Marathon. That summer, She competed in the World Veterans

Marathon Championship in Scotland. She became the first woman in the world to run what's called a "sub-three-hour" (or "under-three-hour") marathon in the over-50 age division. She ran it in 2 hours, 57 minutes and 20 seconds.

Toshiko Kishimoto D'Elia is a very strong and independent woman who has overcome cancer and many other hardships in her life so that she can accomplish her goals. She retired from teaching at the New York School for the Deaf after 36 years. We learned from her that we should try to finish what we start and always do our best. "Be true to your own convictions and responsible to what you believe in."

Reverend Ryo Imamura

Can you imagine what it would be like to be born in a family in which at least one son became a Buddhist priest for 18 generations? This is the case for Reverend Ryo (ree-oh) Imamura's family.

Rev. Imamura (ee-mah-moo-rah) was born in 1944 at the Gila #2 internment camp in Arizona. He spent most of his childhood in Berkeley, California. He remembers his parents telling him he could be whatever he wanted to be. For a while he studied to be a doctor, then he was a high school math teacher. Finally, he decided to become a Buddhist priest, but his parents still told him to really think about it because they wanted him to be happy. He studied at his family temple in Fukui (foo-koo-ee), Japan, and became an ordained Buddhist priest in 1972.

Rev. Imamura is very proud of his heritage now, but he told us that he did not

Rev. Ryo Imamura (second from right)

always feel this way. He has memories of feeling upset about racism as a child. Ever since he was a young kid, he remembers being made to feel he was not good enough to be an American. He remembers playing the game "Bombs Over Tokyo" at recess during school and always being "bombed." He was never asked to play after school with the other kids or invited to their birthday parties. He believes other kids thought he was especially strange because he lived right next door to the Japanese Buddhist temple, which the kids didn't understand.

When he was in the sixth grade, he was elected to be the Top Sergeant of the school traffic patrol by his class. As the Top Sergeant he would be in charge of the older kids who helped the little ones cross the street. He was very surprised at being elected to the most important job in school. So were the school teachers and other grown-ups. They did not expect a Japanese American kid to get this important job.

When Rev. Imamura went to school the day after election, he found out that he had lost his important job. He was told he would be the Quartermaster Sergeant,

instead of Top Sergeant. This was a step down. He was replaced by a white student. The adults told him that his voice was too soft and this was why he couldn't be Top Sergeant. He and his parents did not complain, even though they knew that he didn't get the job because of his race. His family knew that, at the time, fighting back was not a solution because they would not win. Now that he is a Buddhist priest, he helps others understand that everyone should be treated fairly.

If he had to pick the one person who had the biggest influence on his life, it would be his maternal grandmother, Rev. Shinobu Matsuura (maht-soo-rah). She was a Buddhist priest of the Jodo Shin sect, and a poet. He described her as "a little chubby lady who was admired by and loved by countless others around the world." His other grandmother was also a respected figure among Buddhists and was written about in a book about Hawaiian women.

Rev. Imamura's advice to young Japanese Americans is, "Continue the struggle toward wisdom and compassion. Have

pride and confidence in your unique and beautiful selves. And, at the same time, realize the interrelatedness of all beings and strive to bring out the best in others."

Mr. Imamura now lives in Tumwater, Washington, with his wife, Debra, and his two Yonsei sons. He teaches psychology and Buddhism at Evergreen State College in Olympia, Washington. He has a master's degree in counseling and a doctorate (the highest degree you can get) in psychology. He was a counselor for many years and co-founded the East-West Couseling Center in Berkeley, California, which helped mainly the Asian-American community. He finds his job exciting and fulfilling. Rev. Imamura has also been active in the peace and anti-nuclear movement.

We wonder if one of his sons will have the desire to become a Buddhist priest just like his father. He would be the nineteenth generation, more than five hundred years of Buddhist priests in one family!

Dr. Lane Hirabayashi

"Learning about your heritage is very important! This, in turn, helps you appreciate all the things your family did for you. This will give you courage and strength." This is what Dr. Lane Hirabayashi (hee-rah-bah-yah-shee), who is an associate professor of anthropology and Asian American Studies at the University of Colorado, says to younger kids. He was born on October 17, 1952, in Seattle, Washington. He is Sansei, or third generation. Dr. Hirabayashi has parents of different heritages. His mom is Norwegian and his father is Japanese.

Dr. Lane Hirabayashi

This makes him and his younger sister, Jan, half Japanese American. He grew up in Mill Valley, California. It took his parents a long time to find a place to live where there were good schools. Many people would not rent houses to Japanese people in the 1950s.

When he was growing up, his parents thought it was very important to be good and not lie or steal. They also believed in the Golden Rule, which is to "do unto others as you would have them do unto you." They thought education and helping others were very important, too. Dr. Hirabayashi told us he was very happy that his mom shared her love of books and learning with her children.

In the fourth grade, one kid in Dr. Hirabayashi's art class teased him and made fun of his last name. That really upset him. He walked outside, sat on the swings and felt bad. Later, the art teacher told him that she liked his last name and that made him feel better.

Dr. Hirabayashi's heroes changed as he grew up. When he was little, he looked up to the older kids in the neighborhood. When he was in junior high and high school, he liked the musicians James Brown and the Beatles. During this time, he wanted to be a musician and did play in some blues bands in the San Francisco Bay area.

In college, his heroes were his dad, uncle, and grandfather, Shungo (shoon-goh) John Hirabayashi. He remembers his father and uncle telling him about their hard times. In 1922, Shungo John Hirabayashi's land was taken away by the U.S. government because he wasn't allowed to become an American citizen. The family didn't think that was the right thing to do so they went to court to get their land back. The court people felt it *was* the right thing to do, so Shungo John Hirabayashi never got his land back.

During World War II, his uncle Gordon Hirabayashi, who was a Quaker, didn't think it was right or fair that the Japanese Americans had to go into internment camps, so he refused to go. He decided to go to court about it. The Quakers helped him by raising money and supporting his beliefs. When he went to court, the judge didn't agree with him so he was sent to jail in Arizona. They wouldn't pay for the trip, and they didn't care how he got there, so he hitchhiked from Washington all the way to

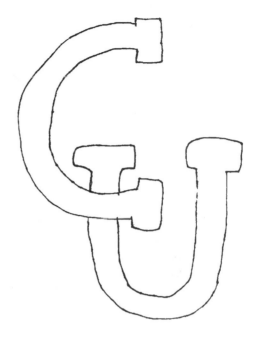

Arizona just to go to jail! He showed he was honest by getting himself to the jail. The things that made Dr. Hirabayashi admire both his grandfather and his uncle were that they fought for equal rights and they didn't give up.

Even though he was a terrible student in high school, Dr. Hirabayashi made up for it in college. He went to universities and got his B.A., M.A., and Ph.D. degrees. Besides teaching at a university, he's also in a neat program which teaches classes and does research about different racial minorities in the U.S. He married his wife, Marilyn, in 1988, and has a stepdaughter, Denise. He believes his family and his work to be the most important things in his life. Also, one of his goals is to write books and he does. His other goal is to be the best person he can be.

Dr. Hirabayashi told us, "By getting the best education that you can and by taking school seriously, you can find out about the world while you discover what you're really good at." We think that's a great lesson to learn and remember!

David Nieda

When David Nieda (nee-eh-dah) was in high school, he went on a silent retreat one day. He was sitting quietly under a tree when he felt God trying to call him. Did God want him to be a minister? David Nieda decided not to answer the call because he wanted to go to college and make lots of money.

Rev. Nieda attended college at the University of California at Los Angeles (UCLA). His calling to money gave him many ideas of what he would like to do. Would he be a lawyer, businessman, disk jockey, newspaper reporter, or teacher? He was getting close to graduation, but he still did not know what he should do.

Once again, he felt God trying to call him. This time Rev. Nieda answered the call and decided to become a minister. He went to the Iliff School of Theology in Denver, Colorado, where he started working with the youth group at a Methodist church. He knew this was important for him to do because he could achieve his goal of helping Japanese American youth have pride in their heritage and learn more about God.

Rev. Nieda works hard every year bringing pride and the love of God to Asian Camp, where he teaches in the summer. It's a summer camp program sponsored by Asian American Methodist churches from

Rev. David Nieda

the Pacific Northwest, California, and Colorado. He told us that students in grade 7 through college spend the week learning about what it means to be Asian American. He also shows them that scripture can be very important in their personal lives. They learn about racism and hunger around the world. They may also participate in a sharing show or even a mini dance competition.

Rev. Nieda is a Nisei Japanese American. Most Nisei ministers are in their fifties and sixties, but Rev. Nieda is young. He was born on January 27, 1964. We think his young age helps him relate to the youth in his church.

If Rev. Nieda could change one thing in our country, it would be to have fairness and justice for everyone in our society. If this happened there would be less racism and more friendship between people of all races.

The most important things in Rev. Nieda's life are his ministry and his identity as a Japanese American. His advice to Japanese American youth is to ask questions and be curious about your heritage and to have a friendship with God. He wants you to be proud of who you are.

Cara Beth Yamaguchi

You might think when you first meet Cara Beth Yamaguchi (yah-mah-goo-chee) that when she was young she was a good student and liked to study. You may be surprised to know that as a young child in school, she did not like to study and couldn't sit still for more than ten minutes. Her teachers were always surprised because they expected her to fit the sterotype of being a good student just because she was Japanese American. Today she is the president of Cellular Distributors, Inc., in Hawaii and she has been honored by the U.S. Small Business Administration because of her successful business.

Ms. Yamaguchi was born February 17, 1965 in Hawaii. She says that her family history is a little bit different from families on the mainland (the main part of the United States). Her grandfather was not put in a camp during World War II. The only thing he had to do was answer a list of questions the government gave to him. She thinks that people in Hawaii were treated differently back then because there were so many

Ms. Cara Beth Yamaguchi in her office

Japanese living there. Ms. Yamaguchi remembers that when she was a little girl her parents had a bomb shelter. During World War II people built bomb shelters made of cement in their back yards. People used them to protect themselves from bombs that might fall in their neighborhood.

Before Ms. Yamaguchi went to college she wanted to be a veterinarian. When she found out she would have to put some animals to sleep, she decided that this wasn't for her. While she was in college, a friend encouraged her to start her own business selling cellular phones. Ms. Yamaguchi had to go to the public library and do research by herself to learn what cellular means and how the phones worked. There wasn't anyone who could train her for the job so she taught herself. She plans to help others in the future by teaching them about cellular phones and small businesses.

Ms. Yamaguchi feels that the way people make fun of others is still the same as when she was young. She feels lucky to have grown up in a Japanese American neigh-

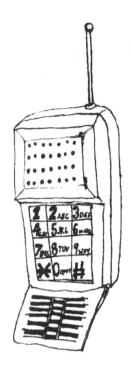

and loving toward each other and towards themselves. This is my wish for the world."

A lot of 26-year-olds are busy partying and having a good time. Mr. Ito is having a good time too, but not like other people! The most important thing in his life is serving others. He wants to make our world a better place to live by serving his family, community, and friends. Mr. Ito thinks he can touch people the most by developing his own talents and sharing them. This feeling led to one of the most important decisions of his life — going to graduate school. He's studying all sorts of things about the Earth because he wants to be a geophysicist. A geophysicist is a scientist who studies what the Earth is made of and how it's changing. He is at the Massachu-

borhood. She told us that being Japanese American has changed her life because her Japanese heritage taught her to value family and friends, and treat others with respect. Since family is so important to her, she was very careful when dating. She met Bryan Yogi, a very kind and patient man, and on July 3, 1993, they were married. She and her husband hope to pass their values on to their family.

The advice she has for youth is to be proud of your heritage, cultures and traditions. It doesn't matter what nationality you are, if you work hard you will achieve your goals.

Garrett Ito

"If I were magic," says Garrett Ito (ee-toh), "I would make people more caring

Mr. Garrett Ito

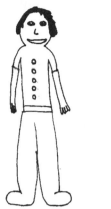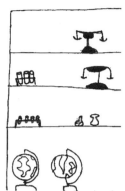

When he was growing up, his family celebrated holidays, especially New Year's Day. Sometimes, in the summer, his mother and sister would dance in the Obon. This is a summer festival where Japanese Americans get together to dance folk dances in celebration of their ancestors. Everyone dresses in traditional summer kimonos called yukata (yoo-kah-tah).

Being Japanese American is something that Mr. Ito is very proud of. When he was a senior in college, he visited Japan and had a wonderful time! He really learned a lot about his grandparents and came to understand and respect their values. He appreciates his Japanese heritage and thinks that being different makes you special. That's what he thinks is neat about America—everyone has a different heritage.

Kimberly Po

Have you ever heard of Kimberly Po? Well, if you haven't, she's a touring tennis pro and she's *really* good! Miss Po lives in Westwood, California, near the UCLA campus. She was born on October 20, 1971, and she's half-Chinese and half-Japanese.

As Miss Po grew up, she did a lot of things with her older brother, Greg, like going to the park and playing games and sports. Her parents thought the Golden Rule (treat others as you would like to be treated) and education were really important. As a child, her family celebrated Japanese and Chinese New Years as well as other holidays.

Miss Po played competitive soccer before she played tennis. Although she enjoyed soccer very much, she sometimes got frus-

setts Institute of Technology in Cambridge, Massachusetts, working on his Ph.D. To get into this school, you have to be VERY smart!

Mr. Ito has lots of heroes! We think this is because he looks for the good in all the people he meets. His first hero was Steve Austin, the main character on *The Six Million Dollar Man* television show. Now his hero is Greg LeMond, who is a famous bicycle racer. He likes riding bikes himself and he respects Greg for all the races he has won.

Mr. Ito was born on March 4, 1967. His family moved to Anaheim, California where he lived until he was thirteen. After that, they moved to Englewood, Colorado, where he lived until he went to college. Besides his mom and dad, he also has a younger sister, Ellyn. When he was little, his parents thought that developing self-esteem, believing in himself, being a hard worker, and having personal values were all very important. This made him want to grow up and make a difference in the world.

Miss Kimberly Po practicing tennis

trated that some players weren't trying as hard as she was. At nine years old, she decided to give tennis a try. By the age of 11 she was playing in national tournaments, and she's been playing ever since.

Miss Po became really good at tennis when she was in high school. In 1987, when she was 16, she ranked #3 for singles and #1 for doubles nationally. She was also in honors classes, which are really hard classes. So, as you can see, she's not only good at tennis, she's good at a lot of other things too.

Miss Po is very glad we are writing this book to fight racism. She has had to face this problem herself. One day, while she was in high school, she was walking to her car when she saw two boys in the back of

a car looking at her and making fun of her eyes. When she saw them, she wanted to go up to that car and tell their mother what the two boys had just done, but she didn't. Miss Po was really shocked, because she thought all the racism was gone, but it wasn't—and still isn't.

Miss Po went to college at UCLA in 1989 for two years before she decided to play tennis professionally. It was a really hard decision, because both tennis and education are important to her.

She wants to play tennis for six or seven more years and then retire from tennis, go back to college, and graduate. Then she wants to go to law school to study environmental law.

She thinks people should be more aware of other people's different backgrounds and respect them. She also thinks it's important to learn about your own heritage and know what your parents and grandparents and great-grandparents did, so you can live a happier life and not go through what they did.

The advice Kimberly Po has for American youth is to learn more about your

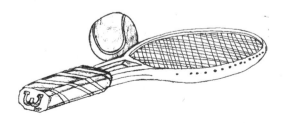

heritage and your family's history. Being both Japanese American and Chinese American has made her more aware of all the other races in the world around her.

Jill Ogawa

Have you ever been teased or bullied? What did you do? What did you say? When Jill Ogawa (oh-gah-wah) was in high school, she had to decide how to handle just such a situation.

Ms. Ogawa was about to serve the ball in a high school volleyball tournament when some fans from the other school started shouting at her. They called her "Jap" and "samurai." She had to decide whether to take a stand or to just continue playing. She decided to stop the game and ask the referee to remove these fans.

At first the referee just laughed, and Ms. Ogawa had to tell her again. Finally, the fans were told to stop, but they were not asked to leave. Ms. Ogawa wondered if she did the right thing, because she interrupted the game. Later, she decided it had been the right thing to do, because the fans were wrong for saying what they did. Ms. Ogawa told us that the important thing to remember is not to take any racial remarks or prejudice sitting down. Stand up for what you believe!

Ms. Ogawa was born on September 22, 1972. She is now in college and wants to be a doctor.

As a child, Ms. Ogawa was very active. She lived near many boys and she played sports with them all the time. When she was three years old, she started taking gymnastics lessons. This was when her parents

Miss Jill Ogawa, lacrosse player

first realized that she might be a good athlete someday.

She played sports all during her teenage years. When she was in high school, she played on the varsity volleyball, basketball, and lacrosse teams. She won many awards, including a Most Valuable Player (MVP) award in volleyball and lacrosse, and honorable mention for All-American for lacrosse. She was captain of her volleyball and lacrosse teams.

People sometimes wonder if they can be good at sports if they are short, but Ms. Ogawa has proved you can be. She has a good sense of humor about her height. She says she is "five feet tall on a good day." Her coaches thought she would have problems competing against taller players, but she believes hard work and never quitting helped her succeed in sports.

Jill Ogawa says going to college will give her more opportunities to have a career. She knows that her education is more important than her participation in sports. She was on the Honor Roll all through high school and was on the Merit List at Kenyon College in Ohio.

Ms. Ogawa goes to a Methodist church where most of the members are Japanese Americans. Here she practices her Christian faith and many Japanese cultural things like origami and Japanese dances.

For many years, she has gone to a Methodist Asian American summer camp. She likes participating in the camp because it is a place where race doesn't matter and she is accepted because of who she is inside. At camp, the kids learn how to handle prejudice and become good friends with other Christians. Ms. Ogawa has learned how important it is to feel good about yourself all the time. She thinks all young people should learn about their own culture and other cultures in America.

HANDS-ON FUN

You can cook, play games, and make crafts, too,
And do things that are fun for you.
You can learn to do things the Japanese way,
And brighten any gloomy day.

In this chapter you will learn how to make some crafts, play some new games, and cook some favorite Japanese American recipes. We thought it was neat to do these things in our workshop, because they have been done by children and adults for hundreds of years. We learned that we have a lot in common with kids from long ago, no matter where we come from.

CRAFTS

Origami

Origami (oh-ree-gah-mee) is the art of paper folding. It started in Japan over six hundred years ago, and many Americans enjoy this hobby today. All you do is follow directions to fold paper many times in different shapes until it turns into what you are trying to make. You learn to concentrate, read and follow directions, and be patient.

When you do origami, you are also learning math and geometry, because you are making shapes while you are folding paper. Origami paper always starts out as a square,

Learning the art of origami

Chris Tucker

Chris Tucker

Having fun with origami hats

and it comes in different colors. One side of the paper is usually white and the other side is either a solid color or a colored design.

Many people like to make cranes out of origami paper, because they are a special symbol for many things. The crane is a symbol of peace and long life. It is also a sign of good health. Some people believe the crane will help make miracles happen and make your dreams come true.

Japanese Americans sometimes give their daughters or sons one thousand cranes in red, gold, or silver when they get married to wish them good luck. The most popular color for wedding cranes is gold. Some families make one thousand gold cranes for a fiftieth wedding anniversary.

When doing origami you get to enjoy the beauty of what you make. It also feels good to finish something and be able to follow directions. Practicing origami can help make the muscles in your fingers stronger and teach you to move them gracefully. We give origami two thumbs up!

There are many books on origami that tell you how to make a crane. After you learn to do this, try making one thousand cranes with your friends or family. Then give them to someone on an important occasion. This would be a good project for a rainy day.

Darumas

The daruma (dah-roo-mah) is a popular Japanese figure, sort of like a little doll. It stands for inner strength, determination, and perseverance. It was named after Bodhidharma (boh-dee-dar-mah), a Zen priest. He sat and meditated for a long, long time. After doing this, he lost the use of his arms and legs. Many legends say that he then rolled himself through China to teach his religion.

The daruma is a little egg-shaped figure with a weight in the bottom so it will pop

back up, kind of like a punching bag. You might think the daruma's face looks angry, but it's not. It's a look of determination.

The daruma is thought to be a good-luck charm against illness and bad fortune. Some people think of a goal they want to achieve. Then they draw the outline of eyes on the daruma but fill in only one eye. When their goal or wish comes true, they fill in the other eye. But for the wish to come true, they have to work hard.

We're glad this idea came from Japan to America. Some of us are painting one eye and our goal is to make good grades. We will keep working, even though it is hard. Just like the daruma, no matter which way you push us, we will pop back up.

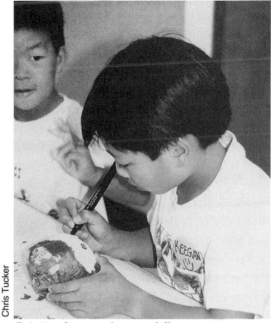

Chris Tucker

Painting faces on daruma dolls

How to Make a Daruma

When you make something, always keep in mind what it will look like in the end. A daruma has the shape of an egg with a flat bottom. Look at the picture and think about what you want yours to look like. To make a daruma you will need a plastic sandwich bag, strips of paper, liquid starch, plaster of paris, and colored paints.

1. To begin, stuff a plastic sandwich bag with strips of crumpled paper until it is very full.
2. Fold the top of the bag over and tape it shut. This is also the time to tape the corners of the bag in and try to form an egg shape with a flat bottom.
3. Draw a 1-inch circle on the very top of the bag. We will cut out this circle later and use the hole to remove the paper.
4. Take a strip of newspaper 1 inch wide

and 6 inches long, and dip it in liquid starch. Wrap it around the plastic bag, but don't cover the hole. Do this again and again until the whole bag is covered with four or five layers of papier mâché.
5. As you put on the layers, remember to work on the shape. Look at the picture to see what shape the daruma has. Make

Chris Tucker

A collection of daruma dolls

certain it is flat on the bottom, so it will stand up.

6. After it has dried overnight, cut out the circle on top and pull out the paper from inside the plastic bag.

7. When all the newspaper is out, pour about a half-inch of plaster of paris in the bottom to make it heavy. Cover the top with more papier mâché and then let it dry until it is hard.

8. When it is dry, paint the face white and the body red. After that has dried, decorate the face with black and gold.

9. Color in one eye and make a wish or set a goal. When your wish comes true or when you have met your goal, color in the other eye.

This project is fun because your daruma makes you try to reach your goal. When both of the eyes are colored in, it helps you remember your success. You might want to make one as a gift for a friend's birthday or graduation.

Kites

Several thousand years ago the very first kite was flown in China. From there the idea soon spread to Japan. The Japanese word for "kite" is *tako* (tah-koh) which also means "octopus." Can you guess why this was chosen for the word "kite"?

People all over the world enjoy flying kites at any time. You can see them in parks, on beaches, open fields, and meadows. Kite flying is a popular sport for all ages, from kids to adults. Today's kites range from the hand-held ones to remote control kites.

Chris Tucker

A Japanese kite

There are giant kites that weigh over 1,700 pounds and take fifty people to fly them. Other kites are as small as postage stamps. Some people even fly as many as five or more kites at the same time. It's fun just to sit and watch beautiful kites soaring gracefully in the sky.

Kites are made out of many different materials but the one thing they have in common is that they are very colorful. We found an easy way to make a kite that really flies. You will need a white plastic trash bag that you can draw a picture on. You might want to draw a picture of a samurai (Japanese warrior), or you can use fairy tale characters, animals, or nature scenes to decorate your kite.

Here are the directions for making a kite:

1. Cut out your kite according to the measurements shown in the picture.
2. Tape two 16-inch dowels (thin, round sticks) to the left and right sides of the trash bag.
3. Make a design or draw a picture with permanent markers so it doesn't rub off. Make your kite colorful.

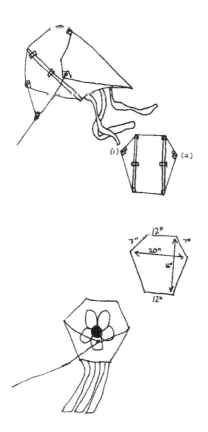

4. Put several pieces of tape on corners (1) and (2) to make them strong.

5. Poke a hole in these corners with something sharp. Be careful not to hurt yourself.

6. Cut a string twice as wide as your kite. In the middle of the string, tie a small loop. Then put the string through the holes you made at (1) and (2) so that the loop is in the middle of one side of the kite.

7. Tie the ends of this string together on the other side of the kite.

8. Tie the end of a long flying string to the little loop in the middle of the string that goes through the holes at (1) and (2).

9. Tape three rag tails or crepe paper strips to the bottom of the kite.

Wait for a windy day and see how easy it is to fly this kite.

Carp Wind Socks

Wind socks are cloth tubes, open at both ends, that hang outside and wave in the wind. In America you can buy wind socks in many different shapes and sizes. In recent years they have become very popular and can be seen flying from balconies, porches, and patios. Carp wind socks might be seen during a Japanese American festival.

The carp is a fish that is important in Japanese culture. Read the Boys' Day section in the chapter about Culture and the Arts to learn the legend of a boy named Kintaro and how he fought with a man-eating carp. You'll also find out why families will fly several carp wind socks of different sizes on Boys' Day.

We think wind socks are fun and easy to make. Here's how to make a carp wind sock.

You will need some cloth. Old white sheets or muslin are best. You will also need scissors, thread or fabric glue, markers or felt pens in different colors, a pipe cleaner, wax paper, and string.

1. Cut your cloth in the shape of a carp. See the picture on the next page.

2. Make a 1-inch fold at the flat tip of the carp, insert a pipe cleaner in the fold, and then glue the mouth of the carp with the pipe cleaner still in the fold.

3. Fold your carp in half the long way. Then twist the ends of the pipe cleaner together. Insert wax paper in between the fold so that the paint won't go through onto the

Chris Tucker

Making a carp wind sock

other side. Glue or sew the edges of the carp together, leaving the mouth and tail section open so the wind can get inside. 4. Decorate your carp using felt pens or poster paint. You can decorate your wind sock with paint brushes or sponges cut in a kidney shape (to sponge-paint the scales).

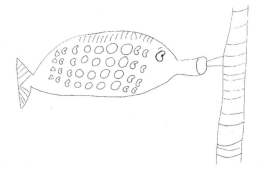

Use any extra material to make fins or streamers on the end.

5. When your design is dry, tie a heavy string to the mouth so your carp can fly.

The best part about making a carp wind sock was decorating it. We could be as creative as we wanted to be. When they were displayed, we knew exactly which one was ours.

GAMES

In this section, you will find games you play the Japanese American way. We played these games and think you will like them.

Go

Go (goh) is a Japanese game that is very enjoyable. *Go* means "five" in Japanese. In Japan, it is the most popular indoor game, and it can be very complex. It is played by some Japanese American children. We played Go and liked it.

This is how to play Go. You have a rectangular board 20 inches by 19 inches, set up with 19 lines up and down and 19 lines across to make a checkerboard. Two people take turns putting tokens on the board at any point where the line cross, until one gets five in a row.

The rows can be in any direction. As you play you try to block the other person from getting five in a row first. Go is like the game Connect Four. The only thing different is that you have to get four in a row instead of five. Like Connect Four and Tic Tac Toe, you have to think fast and use different strategies to play Go.

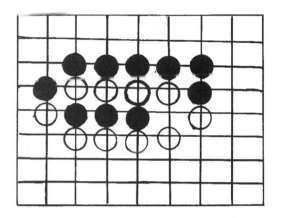

Bean Go

Bean Go is like Go. You use the same board and the same tokens, but in Bean Go you put your tokens inside the squares and then surround the other person's tokens. While you play, your partner tries to surround your tokens. Once you surround the other person's tokens, you take them. The winner is the person who gets all of the other player's tokens.

Young authors learning to play Bean Go

Jan Ken Po

Have you ever played the game "rock, scissors, paper"? Well, there is a Japanese American game called Jan Ken Po (jahn kehn poh) that is very similar to it. Instead of "1, 2, 3!", you say "Jan Ken Po," which is a way to decide whose turn is next, sort of like "eenie, meenie, minie, moe." The name of the game comes from *ken*, which means "fist." Here are the directions.

Pick out a friend to play this game with you. Shake your fist three times in the air. The first time you shake your fist, say "Jan." The second time, say "Ken." The last time,

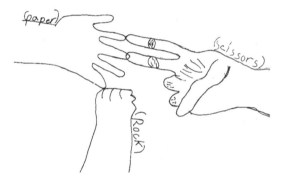

say "Po," and make a fist for rock, open hand for paper, or a V for scissors. The way to find out who wins is: The rock breaks the scissors, the paper covers the rock, and the scissors cut the paper.

Hashi Kyoso

To play Hashi Kyoso (hah-shee kyoh-soh), you will need a cup for each player, hashi (chopsticks), and something to pick up, like peanuts or marshmallows. You will need two or more people to play. The idea is to have a contest to see who can get all the marshmallows out of the cup first by getting one out at a time using only the hashi

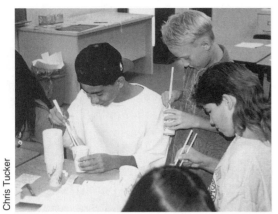

Chris Tucker

Playing Hashi Kyoso

(no poking holes). This game will be easier if you learn to use the hashis by reading the section under "Recipes" called "How to Use Hashi."

Another good way to play this game is to see who can eat the marshmallows (or peanuts) faster. Anyone can play this game. The point of this game is to teach you to use hashis. It is lots of fun.

RECIPES

Japanese Americans believe that food should look good *and* taste good. Each serving is put in a separate dish to keep the taste from running together. Japanese American cooking usually uses the freshest ingredients and cooks them for only a short time. The recipes also use meat in small amounts. This way of cooking is said to be one of the healthiest ways of cooking in the world.

The most common food is rice. Noodles are also enjoyed. We liked all the different kinds of noodles. *Soba* (soh-bah) are brown noodles made from buckwheat. *Udon* (oo-dohn), or winter noodles, and *somen* (soh-men), or summer noodles, are both made from wheat flour. These noodles may be served hot or cold. The noodles can be eaten as a quick snack, just like an apple or a sandwich. Many soybean products are used, such as soy sauce, *miso* (mee-soh) (soybean paste), and *tofu* (toh-foo), which is soybean curd. These are an important part of Japanese American cooking.

The recipes included in this section show the importance of the changing of the seasons. These recipes are easy to prepare and the ingredients can be found easily. The average cooking time for the recipes is about 45 minutes.

Other recipes, such as *teriyaki*, *sashimi* (sah-shee-mee) (raw fish), and *tempura* (vegetables or seafood fried in a special batter), were not included, because they are too hard for kids to make or cost too much money.

Even though cooking the food is fun, eating it is the best part! We would like to

Chris Tucker

Learning to cook Japanese American recipes

teach you how to use hashi (chopsticks) to eat your food. Some people don't know there is a difference between Japanese and Chinese chopsticks. Japanese hashi are smaller and thinner than Chinese chopsticks. If you want a fun way to practice using hashi, play the game Hashi Kyoso from the games section.

How to Use Hashi

1. Rest one of the hashi between your middle finger and thumb. Curl your index (pointer) finger over the top. It's kind of like using a pencil.

2. Pinch the other hashi between your index finger and thumb. Push your index finger down and keep the bottom hashi straight with your thumb. Keep the hashi ends even.

3. Chow down! Enjoy!

Dashi

Dashi (dah-shee) is a soup base for many dishes in Japanese American cooking. Many recipes start with dashi. Dashi is used for all Japanese American noodles. You will find that you will use this recipe frequently while cooking.

6 cups water
5-6 teaspoons *hon dashi* (hohn
  dah-shee) (concentrated soup base)
Boil water. Add hon dashi. Stir.

Somen

Somen, also called summer noodles, is very good as a main dish or as a snack. You can eat this with chopsticks or a fork. Somen noodles are good in the summertime, especially when the weather is hot, because they are cold and can cool you off. This recipe is really easy. It serves eight people.

Somen Noodles

2 lbs. somen noodles

Toppings: green onions, *kamaboko* (kah-mah-boh-koh) (pressed fish cake), hard boiled eggs, *nori* (noh-ree) (dried seaweed), or cucumber.

In a large saucepan, bring water to a boil. Add somen noodles. Cook 3 minutes. Do not overcook. Drain in a colander and run cold water over them. Set aside. You also need somen sauce for this dish.

Somen Sauce

6 cups dashi
½ cup *mirin* (mee-reen) (Japanese
  sweet rice wine used for cooking)
½ cups shoyu (soy sauce)

In a large saucepan, combine all ingre-

dients. Boil mixture and then refrigerate sauce until you're ready to serve the noodles. To serve, put noodles in small bowls and pour some sauce over them, then add toppings.

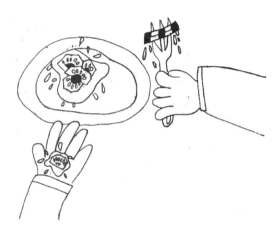

Sunomono

Sunomono (soo-noh-moh-noh) is cucumber salad. This dish has both a sweet and salty taste to it. Many of us kids liked the mix of sugar and salt together. The sauce is a mixture of soy sauce, rice vinegar, and sugar. This recipe is easy to make and doesn't take much time. It serves four people.

    2 cucumbers, sliced thin
    ¼ cup sugar
    ¼ cup rice vinegar
    ¼ teaspoon salt
    ¼ teaspoon shoyu (soy sauce)

Cut off ends of the cucumber. Peel the cucumber in alternating stripes, then slice it. Sprinkle the cucumber with salt and set aside. Mix remaining ingredients to make vinegar mixture. Rinse cucumbers with cold water. Squeeze out excess water. Add to vinegar mixture.

Okazu

When you are really hungry, you should try this dish. It is called *okazu* (oh-kah-zoo) and is mixed vegetables and meat. It is usually served with rice. It makes a good meal any day of the week and uses up what is in the refrigerator. Maybe you could treat your family by cooking this for dinner. Remember to ask your parents for permission. This recipe serves four people.

Chris Tucker

Young chefs at work

½ lb. sliced meat (beef, pork, ground
beef, chicken)
½ lb. tofu
any combination of sliced vegetables:
   green onions
   nappa (Chinese cabbage)
   mushrooms
   green beans
   green peppers

This is a very easy recipe, because all you
have to do is fry everything up in a frying
pan and then add water, a little shoyu,
and sugar to your desired taste. Serve okazu
on rice or noodles for a tasty dinner.

Rice

Rice is the most popular food for both
Japanese Americans and Japanese. It is
eaten by millions of people all over the
world. The name for cooked rice is

gohan (goh-hahn). This word also means
"a full meal."

3 cups rice
3½ cups water

Wash and rinse the rice until the water
is almost clear. Drain off all the water in the
last wash. Pour in the measured amount of
water. Cover and cook in a rice cooker or
on the stove. Let it steam for 10 minutes
after it is finished cooking. If you cook it on
the stove, use a deep pan. Cook the rice
at a high heat until it begins to almost boil
over (the pan lid should be bouncing up
and down). Lower the heat as low as possible and simmer for 15 minutes. Let the
rice stand for 10 minutes and then use a
wooden spoon or spatula to fluff it up.

Spam Nigiri

If you like meat and rice, then you will like
Spam *nigiri* (nee-gee-ree). It is a popular
snack in Hawaii. Spam is the meat in this
recipe. It tasted different and good.

1 sheet nori (dried seaweed)
1 cup cooked rice (see above)
Spam (large can, cut into 12 ½-inch-long
   strips)

Cook Spam in frying pan (optional: add
teriyaki sauce). Cut nori in half. Put a half
cup of rice on each piece of nori. Spread
rice out. Salt to taste. Leave one inch at
edge of nori plain (or without rice) to seal
roll. Place Spam on top of rice and roll up
the nori.

Onigiri

Onigiri (oh-nee-gee-ree) are rice balls. Here is how you make them:

1. Wet your hands slightly and place a little salt on your hands.
2. Scoop a handful of rice and form into ovals, balls, or triangles. You can also use wood or plastic molds to form the shapes.
3. They're ready to eat!

If you want to make this look pretty, you could add seasoned nori (seaweed) or sesame seeds.

Shoyu Weiners

Shoyu weiners are a delicious Japanese American food that is easy to cook. They are hot dogs cooked in soy sauce. This recipe serves five people.

5 weiners
3 tablespoons of shoyu (soy sauce)
2 tablespoons of sugar

Chris Tucker

Authors making onigiri

Slice the weiners diagonally, about ¼-inch thick. Fry them in a little oil. Add shoyu and sugar. Stir until weiners are coated. Serve hot.

Rolled Sukiyaki

This is a great-tasting Japanese American meal of meat and vegetables. It's easy to make and fun to eat.

½ lb. green beans
½ lb. *sukiyaki* (soo-kee-yah-kee) meat (thinly sliced beef)

First, boil the green beans for a very short time. Place them in a colander and drain.

Cut the sukiyaki meat in half the short way. Next place two or three string beans on the meat and roll it up. Brown the meat rolls in a skillet, turning them carefully. Pour teriyaki sauce over them.

Teriyaki Sauce

Teriyaki sauce is used a lot in Japanese American cooking. Here is how you make it.

¼ cup sugar
¼ cup soy sauce
1 teaspoon cornstarch mixed with 1
    teaspoon water
Mix all ingredients together.

Miso Shiru

Miso shiru (mee-soh shee-roo) may not sound good to you, but it is. This soup is good even on hot days. Miso shiru is served first at family meals, but last at formal dinners.

6 cups dashi (soup base)
½ lb. tofu (soybean curd), cut into
    small cubes
½ cup miso paste (soybean paste)
green onions (optional)

Put the dashi in a pan and heat it until it boils. Turn down the heat. Dissolve the miso paste in the dashi and add tofu. You can add green onions if desired. This serves six people who aren't too hungry.

Udon

Udon (oo-dohn) noodles are big fat noodles, also called "winter noodles." You serve them hot, with a udon sauce on top. Udon

Chris Tucker

Slicing ingredients for rolled sukiyaki

noodles are good in the wintertime, especially when the weather is cold. This recipe serves four people.

Noodles

1 lb. of Udon noodles

In a large saucepan, bring water to boil. Add noodles and stir. Bring water to a boil again, then add ½ cup cold water. Boil for 6 to 8 minutes. Test for tenderness. Remove from heat, and drain. Run cold water over

noodles. Before serving, pour hot water over noodles.

Sauce

6 cups dashi (soup base)
1 teaspoon salt (optional)
⅓ cup shoyu (soy sauce)
2 teaspoons sugar
2 teaspoons mirin (sweet rice wine)

In a large saucepan combine dashi, salt, shoyu, sugar, and mirin. Heat until hot but not boiling. Remove from heat.

To serve, put noodles in bowls, pour sauce on top, then add toppings for a good flavor. Toppings: kamaboko (pressed fish cake), green onion, and sliced boiled eggs.

Yaki Soba

Yaki soba (yah-kee soh-bah) are stir-fried noodles with meat, carrots, cabbages, or other vegetables. Yaki soba is easy to make and tastes really good. It can be served as a snack or a meal.

1½ tablespoons oil
½ lb. pork or beef, cut thin
¼ head of cabbage
1¼ pound package of fresh or dried yaki soba noodles
4 tablespoons *tonkatsu* (tohn-kah-tsoo) sauce (seasoned sauce)
1 tablespoon shoyu (soy sauce)
1 carrot, cut in slivers
salt and pepper

Heat half the oil in a frying pan and sauté the meat and vegetables over medium heat for two to three minutes until tender. Season with salt and pepper. Remove from heat and set aside. Heat the remaining oil and fry noodles three minutes over medium heat. (If dried noodles are used, cook in boiling water until soft, then drain. Fry noodles in oil.) Add meat and vegetables. Season with tonkatsu sauce and shoyu. Fry about two minutes longer and serve.

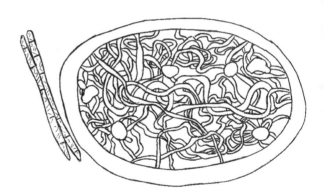

OUR VISION FOR A BETTER WORLD

As we were writing and working on this book, one of the important things we learned was about the practice of stereotyping. Stereotyping is when you look at someone and think you know them just by their race or outside appearance.

Sometimes stereotypes fit, but usually they don't. If you think you know a person just by looking at them, you are probably wrong. You have to get to know them by talking and playing with them.

Here are some things we, the Japanese-American participants in the workshop, wrote to show we are "real people," too. You might find that we have a lot in common.

I am Japanese American. Something about me I want you to know is . . .

. . . I would like to live in the mountains and have a big house with a lot of land and two horses.

. . . I like to dance. When I dance I can let go of all the stress I have collected during the day.

. . . I don't speak much Japanese, and I don't know a lot about the country of Japan.

. . . I feel good about being myself because even though I'm different in many ways, I'm like other people, too.

. . . I'm always glad to learn more about my culture.

. . . My favorite subject in school is reading, and I like to read about many different things.

. . . I am good in math. I feel good to be Japanese American.

Chris Tucker

Young authors taking a break

Chris Tucker

Sharing lunch with friends

. . . I love art.

. . . I feel hurt when I get made fun of at school because I'm Japanese American. People shouldn't make fun just because I'm different.

. . . I like the Japanese American values of respecting other people, enjoying the arts, and thinking that school is one of the most important things in life.

. . . I'm good at judo. I took first place at the Junior Olympics in Michigan.

. . . My favorite food is Mexican food, especially cheese enchiladas.

. . . My favorite food is pizza.

. . . I eat more American food than Japanese food.

. . . I am glad that I am Japanese American, but I don't like it when people make fun of our food, our culture, or me.

. . . I like basketball. My favorite teams are the Bulls, Magic, Lakers, and Hornets.

. . . My hobbies are collecting comic books and CDs.

. . . I'm having fun learning about my heritage and ancestry.

. . . I like it when my grandpa tells me about when he lived in Japan.

. . . I'm 12 years old. I have samurai on both sides of my family. My grandpa went to an internment camp and my grandma had to move to Colorado.

. . . I feel hurt when I hear about the awful discrimination that my grandparents, parents, and relatives endured.

. . . I wish others would judge me like anyone else. I think that it is really unfair to judge people by how they look and their ethnic background.

. . . I want people to know that Japanese Americans are Americans, not Japanese. They are born in America.

. . . I am half African American. I didn't know much about my Japanese American heritage, but I am learning a lot about it now.

. . . I am Buddhist. I am Yonsei, or fourth generation. On my dad's side, I am part Irish and Swedish.

. . . I don't like people to call me "Jap."

. . . I can play taiko drums and do origami, and I go to the Denver Buddhist Temple every Sunday. I used to be one of the only Asian people in my school, but more are beginning to come.

. . . I can write some of the Japanese alphabet, and I can read and speak a little bit of the Japanese language.

. . . I want to learn more about my heritage.

. . . I'm proud to be Japanese American!

Here are some of the things that we, the non-Japanese American authors, learned while writing this book:

. . . Japanese Americans have faced tough times, like during wartime. The government thought that the Japanese Americans were spics, and people said mean things to them.

. . . Japanese Americans were taken away from their homes and put into internment camps.

. . . When you see someone that's different because they're handicapped, they're from a different heritage, or they have problems, treat them the same as you would treat your best friend.

. . . Japanese Americans have been very loyal to their country. Even while their parents were put in internment camps, sons fought for the United States in World War II.

. . . I learned about the different generations of Japanese Americans.

. . . Japanese really like to have their food look good.

. . . Americans come in all different kinds and love their country very much. Looking different doesn't change that.

. . . Many people are treated very badly and if we try hard, we can change the way we treat each other.

. . . Japanese Americans are just like you and me.

WESTRIDGE YOUNG WRITERS WORKSHOP PARTICIPANTS

STUDENT AUTHORS

Zachery Arnone
Justin D. Boehm
James V. Boutwell
Shannon C. Boutwell
Zachary A. Brown
Alyssa Kelly Burnell
Kimberly Lynn Burnell
Jon Isao Campbell
Nicholas Kiyoshi Campbell
Scott S. Chikuma
Holly Kay Clark
Jesse Cowand
Nichole I. Cox
Tara Liana Dell
Dustin DeWitt
Dara Reiko Domoto
Drew Tsutomu Domoto
Isaac Edwards
Kevin Everson
Connarty M. Fagan
Jared J. Fukunaga
Linsay A. Fukunaga
Jessica Erin Funk
Bryce Soichi Fushimi

Desiree Hatsumi
  Fushimi
Keegan Yoichi
  Fushimi
Dan Gorton
Christopher R. Hale
Becky K. Hamada
Sarah Louise
  Heinrich
Tomiko Cim
  Herder
Christopher Shigeo
  Holland
Kimberly Akiko
  Horiuchi
Geoffrey Hikaru Ida
Kenji Kamibayashi
Kimiko Sara Kano
Matthew Kazuo Kawakami
Andrea C. Kelly
Thomas Payton Knight
Heather Anne Krohn
Andrea Nicole Lowe
Kristin MacCary
Michael Manning
José A. Martinez, III
Ray Christopher Maruyama

The authors

Skye Akiko
  Masaki
Akiko Miyake-
  Stoner
Mary Agnes
  Moore
Austin LaMar
  Mori
Lukas Hideo Mori
Mario Yuzo Nieto
Amber Kikuye
  Noguchi
Akihiro Kevin
  Okamoto

Larry Ray Ornelas
Patricia R. Ornelas
Sandra Marie Ornelas
Janine R. Ota
Courtney Akemi Ozaki
Keiko Ann Ozaki
Margaret Tamiko Ozaki
Shannon Masako Ozaki
Neha Pall
Jeremy C. Patterson
Joey L. Pettit
Josh J. Pettit
Jackie Pilling
Deborah Lynne Rhodes
Jessie Rickard
Alexi Rothschild
Zachary Rothschild
Kathryn Morishige Rowen
Harold Sampson, Jr.
Leslie Akimi Sasa
Cathryn M. Shibata
Robert P. Shibata
Chance Matthew Siegele
Chase Michael Siegele
Dirk James Sisneros
Drew Thomas Sisneros
Stefanie Southall

The authors

Erika Sullivan
Joseph Mark Suyeishi
Fumi Takase
Janel Lynette Uyeda
Courtney Nicole Ward
Brandon Weaver
Jared Wertz
Nicole Wessels
Melissa Michiko Whittall
Joloni Shane Williams
Andrew Thomas Wong
Jason Michael Wong
Jennifer Aiko Wong

TEACHERS

Roxanne Carlson Boat
Janice Sayo Campbell
Lisa Caricato
Sue Chichester
Patricia Hagerty Coats
Judith H. Cozzens, Director
Michelle Michiko Crocket
Sandie Dell
Nancy Domoto
Eddie Katsumoto Ellington
Jane Fujioka
Sandy Fukunaga
Mary Ann Garcia-Pettit
Jo-Anne Ginther
Lorraine Gutierrez
Helen Cozzens
    Healy, Co-Director
Brenda F. Hale
Yoshiye Hamada

Jane Hilbert
Donna Inouye
    Holland
Peggy Imatani
Diane Iwersen
Robbin Kitashima
Melissa R.
    Lobach
Annette M.
    Acevedo-
    Martinez
Trudy Ogawa
Judy Natsuko
    Okamoto
Annetta Ornelas
Amy S. Pound
Pat Rhodes
Carolyn Takeshita
Katy Tobo
Sandy Tsubokawa Whittall
Bobbi Shinto Wong

The high school mentors

MENTORS

These high school and college mentors assisted with the writing program and helped in many ways.

Kirsten Frederiksen-Cherry
Shelly Fujikawa
Kiku Lyn Herder
Beth Hitztaler
Aaron Horiuchi
Claire Imatani
Emily Imatani
Jon Kusumi
Kim Lantz
Ryan Lantz
Keith Masaki
Lukas Hideo Mori
David Namura
Paul Namura
Natal Newhouse
Stuart Ota
Lisa Okamoto
Kim Wada
Jennnifer Wanifuchi
Zeni Whittall
Tonia Young

The teachers (sensei)

GLOSSARY OF JAPANESE WORDS

ahiru (ah-hee-roo)–duck

bachi (bah-chee)–sticks used to play taiko and samisen

Bodhidharma (boh-dee-dar-mah)–a Zen priest who took his teachings to China

Bon (bohn), also *Obon* (oh- bohn)–a Buddhist festival to welcome spirits of the dead

Bon-Odori (bohn oh-doh-ree)–an Obon dance

Bonen kai (boh-nehn kye)–a year-end party

bonsai (bohn-sigh)–the art of raising miniature plants and trees with unusually shaped branches

buta (boo-tah)–pig

daikon (dy-kohn)–radish

dana (dah-nah)–selfless giving

dahns (dahns)–steps in the black-belt rank

daruma (dah-roo-mah)–an egg-shaped doll-like Japanese figure

dashi (dah-shee)–a soup base

do itashimashite (doh ee-tah-shee-mahsh-teh)–you're welcome

dojo (doh-joh)–a martial arts school

domo arigato gozaimasu (doh-moh ah-ree-gah-toh goh-zah-ee-mahs)–thank you

furoshiki (foo-roh-shee-kee)–a scarf with a Japanese design

futon (foo-tohn)–a type of bed

gaman (gah-mahn)–tough it out

genki desu (gehn-kee dehs)–I'm fine

genki desu ka (gehn-kee dehs-ka)–how are you?

geta (geh-tah)–Japanese wooden sandals

gi (gee, with a hard "g")–a white uniform worn to do martial arts

giri (gee-ree)–obligation

Go (goh)–a Japanese board game

go (goh)–five

gohan (goh-hahn)–cooked rice, a full meal

gomen nasai (goh-mehn nah-sigh)–I'm sorry

Gosei (goh-say)–fifth generation

hachi (hah-chee)–eight

hachimaki (hah-chee-mah-kee)–a headband

Hachisei (hah-chee-say)–eighth generation

haiku (hy-koo)–a 17-syllable poem

happi (hah-pee)–a kimono coat

Harugakita (hah-roo-gah-kee-tah)–a name of a dance and song

hashi (hah-shee)–chopsticks

Hashi Kyoso (hah-shee kyoh-soh)–a Japanese game played with chopsticks

Hassei (hah-say)–eighth generation

Hina Matsuri (hee-nah mah-tsoo-ree)–annual Girls' Day, Doll Festival

Hina Ningyo (hee-nah neen-gyoh)–miniature dolls that represent the Imperial Court of Japan 300 years ago

hina-dan (hee-nah dahn)–a doll stand

hiragana (hee-rah-gah-nah)–a type of Japanese writing used for everyday use

hitsuji (hee-tsoo-jee)–sheep

hon dashi (hohn dah-shee)–a concentrated soup base

ichi (ee-chee)–one

ikebana (ee-keh-dah-nah)–the art of flower arranging

ikimasho (ee-kee-mah-shoh)–let's go

ikkyu (ee-kyoo)–the first level in *judo*

inu (ee-noo)–dog

Issei (ees-say)–first generation

Jan Ken Po (jahn kehn poh)–a Japanese American game similar to "rock, scissors, paper"

ju (joo)–ten

judo (joo-doh)–a type of martial art, means "the gentle way"

Jusei (joo-say)–tenth generation

kachi-kachis (kah-chee kah-chees)– wooden instruments clicked between two fingers like castanets

kaeru (kah-eh-roo)–frog

kamaboko (kah-mah-bok-koh)–pressed fish cake

kanashi (kah-nah-shee)–I'm sad

kanji (kan-jee)–a type of Japanese formal writing

kansha (kahn-shah)–gratitude toward parents and ancestors

karaoke (kah-rah-oh-keh)–singing on stage along with a tape

karate (kah-rah-tee)–a type of martial art

kata (kah-tah)–several offensive and defensive movements in *karate*

katakana (kah-tah-kah-nah)–a type of Japanese writing used for words that are not originally Japanese

kendo (kehn-doh)–Japanese fencing, a type of martial art

ken (kehn)–a Japanese prefecture

kenjinkai (kehn-jeen-kye)–a group for people from the same *ken*

kibi dango (kee-bee dahn-goh)–rice dumplings

kimono (kee-mohn-noh)–a long robe, means "the thing worn"

kombu (kohm-boo)–seaweed used in cooking

konban wa (kohn-bahn wah)–good evening

konnichi wa (kohn-nee-chee wah)– good day

koto (koh-toh)–a plucked string instrment

ku (koo)–nine

kuro mame (koo-roh mah-meh)–black beans

Kyoto (kyoh-toh)–a city in Japan

Kyusei (kyoo-say)–ninth generation

mirin (mee-reen)–Japanese sweet rice wine used for cooking

miso (mee-soh)–soybean paste

miso shiru (mee-soh shee-roo)–a kind of soup

mochi tsuki (moh-chee tsoo-kee)– sweet rice ball

Moribana (moh-ree-bah-nah)–a style of *ikebana*

mukashi banashi (moo-kah-shee bah-nah-shee)–Japanese folk tales

Nage no Kata (nah-geh noh kah-tah)–a set of 15 different throws in *judo*

Nageire (nah-geh-ee-reh)–a style of *ikebana*

naginata (nah-gee-nah-tah)–a martial art

Nansei (nahn-say)–seventh generation

nappa (nah-pah)–Chinese cabbage

neko (neh-koh)–cat

nezumi (neh-zoo-mee)–mouse

ni (nee)–two

Nihongakko (nee-hohn-gah-koh)–Japanese language school

nikkyu (nee-kyoo)– the second level in *judo*

Nisei (nee-say)–second generation

nishime (nee-shee-meh)–a vegetable dish

nori (noh-ree)–dried seaweed

obento (oh-behn-toh)–a packed lunch in a special lunch box

obi (oh-bee)–a sash worn with a kimono

Obon (oh-bohn), also *Bon* (bohn)–a Buddhist festival to welcome spirits of the dead

ohayo gozaimasu (oh-hah-yo goh-zah-ee-mahs)–good morning

okazu (oh-kah-zoo)–mixed vegetables and meat

ondori (ohn-doh-ree)–rooster

onigiri (oh-nee-gee-ree)–rice balls

origami (oh-ree-gah-mee)–the art of paper folding

Oshogatsu (oh-shoh-gah-tsoo)–New Year's Day

oyasumi nasai (o-yah-soo-mee nah-sye)–good night

ozoni (oh-zoh-nee)–a type of soup

Rikka (ree-kah)–a style of *ikebana*

Rokusei (roh-koo-say)–sixth generation

roku (ro-koo)–six

s'kosh (s'kohsh)–a little bit

sachiko (sah-chee-koh)–happiness

sake (sah-keh)–rice wine

sakura (sah-koo-rah)–cherry blossoms

samisen (sah-mee-sehn)–traditional Japanese stringed instrument similar to a banjo

samurai (sah-moo-rye)–warrior

san (sahn)–three

sankyu (sahn-kyoo)–the third level in *judo*

Sansei (sahn-say)–third generation

Sashimi (sah-shee-mee)–raw fish

sayonara (sah-yoh-nah-rah)–good-bye

sei (say)–generation or an age

sensei (sehn-say)–teacher

shakuhachi (shah-koo-hah-chee)–an instrument made of bamboo, with finger holes, like a flute

shi (shee)–four

shichi (shee-chee)–seven

shiro (shee-roh)–white

shodo (shoh-doh)–Japanese calligraphy

shoji (shoh-jee)–sliding doors with white squares of paper in them

Shoka (shoh-kah)–a style of *ikebana*

shoyu (shoh-yoo) soy sauce

soba (soh-bah)–brown noodles made from buckwheat

somen (soh-men)–summer noodles made from wheat flour

sukiyaki (soo-kee-yah-kee)–meal of meat and vegetables

sumi (soo-mee)–an ink stick used in sumi-e

sumi-e (soo-mee-eh)–the art of ink painting

sunomono (soo-noh-moh-noh)–cucumber salad

tabi (tah-bee)–a type of Japanese sock worn with a kimono

taiko (ty-koh)–an ancient form of drumming

tako (tah-koh)–kite, also mean octopus

Tango No Sekku (tahn-goh noh seh-koo)–Boys' Day

Tanko Bushi (tahn-koh boo-shee)–a folk dance

tatami (tah-tah-mee)–a mat

tempura (tehm-poo-rah)–deep-fried vegetables or seafood

tengu (tehn-goo)–goblin children

tofu (toh-foo)–soybean curd

tonkatsu (tohn-kah-tsoo)–seasoned sauce

tori (toh-ree)–bird

torii (toh-ree-ee)–a wooden gateway with two columns and a cross bar on top

tsukemono (tsoo-keh-moh-noh)–pickled vegetables

Udon (oo-dohn)–winter noodles made from wheat flour

ureshi (oo-reh-shee)–I'm happy

ushi (oo-shee)–cow

yaki soba (yah-kee soh-bah)–stir-fried noodles with meat and vegetables

Yonsei (yohn-say)–fourth generation

yukata (yoo-kah-tah)–summer cotton kimonos

zori (zoh-ree)–thongs

INDEX

BOOKS FOR YOUNG READERS AGES 8 AND UP

from John Muir Publications

X-ray Vision Series

Each title in the series is 8½" x 11", 48 pages, $9.95 paperback, with four-color photographs and illustrations and written by Ron Schultz.

Looking Inside the Brain
Looking Inside Cartoon Animation
Looking Inside Caves and Caverns
Looking Inside Sports Aerodynamics
Looking Inside Sunken Treasure
Looking Inside Telescopes and the
  Night Sky

Masters of Motion Series

Each title in the series is 10¼" x 9", 48 pages, $9.95 paperback, with four-color photographs and illustrations.

How to Drive an Indy Race Car
How to Fly a 747
How to Fly the Space Shuttle

The Extremely Weird Series

All of the titles are written by Sarah Lovett, 8½" x 11", 48 pages, and $9.95 paper.

Extremely Weird Bats
Extremely Weird Birds
Extremely Weird Endangered Species
Extremely Weird Fishes
Extremely Weird Frogs
Extremely Weird Insects
Extremely Weird Mammals
Extremely Weird Micro Monsters
Extremely Weird Primates
Extremely Weird Reptiles
Extremely Weird Sea Creatures
Extremely Weird Snakes
Extremely Weird Spiders

Rainbow Warrior Artists Series

Each title is written by Reavis Moore with a foreword by LeVar Burton, and is 8½" x 11", 48 pages, $14.95 hardcover, with color photographs and illustrations.

Native Artists of Africa
Native Artists of North America
Native Artists of Europe

The Kids Explore Series

Each title is written by kids for kids by the Westridge Young Writers Workshop, 7" x 9", with photographs and illustrations by the kids.

Kids Explore America's Hispanic Heritage
112 pages, $9.95 paper
Kids Explore America's African American Heritage
128 pages, $9.95 paper
Kids Explore the Gifts of Children With Special Needs
128 pages, $9.95 paper
Kids Explore America's Japanese American Heritage
144 pages, $9.95 paper

Bizarre & Beautiful Series

Each title is 8½" x 11", 48 pages, $14.95 hardcover, with four-color photographs and illustrations.

Bizarre & Beautiful Ears
Bizarre & Beautiful Eyes
Bizarre & Beautiful Feelers
Bizarre & Beautiful Noses
Bizarre & Beautiful Tongues

Rough and Ready Series

Each title is 48 pages, 8½" x 11", $12.95 hardcover, with two-color illustrations and duo-tone archival photographs.

Rough and Ready Cowboys
Rough and Ready Prospectors
Rough and Ready Homesteaders
Rough and Ready Railroaders
Rough and Ready Loggers
Rough and Ready Outlaws and Lawmen

American Origins Series

Each title is 48 pages, 8½" x 11", $12.95 hardcover, with two-color illustrations and duo-tone archival photographs.

Tracing Our German Roots
Tracing Our Irish Roots
Tracing Our Italian Roots
Tracing Our Jewish Roots
Tracing Our Chinese Roots
Tracing Our Japanese Roots
Tracing Our Polish Roots

The Kidding Around Travel Guides

All of the titles listed below are 64 pages and $9.95 except for *Kidding Around the National Parks* and *Kidding Around Spain*, which are 108 pages and $12.95.

Kidding Around Atlanta
Kidding Around Boston, 2nd ed.
Kidding Around Chicago, 2nd ed.
Kidding Around the Hawaiian Islands
Kidding Around London
Kidding Around Los Angeles
Kidding Around the National Parks of the Southwest
Kidding Around New York City, 2nd ed.
Kidding Around Paris
Kidding Around Philadelphia
Kidding Around San Diego
Kidding Around San Francisco
Kidding Around Santa Fe
Kidding Around Seattle
Kidding Around Spain
Kidding Around Washington, D.C., 2nd ed.

Environmental Titles

Habitats
8½" x 11", 48 pages, color illustrations, $9.95 paper

The Indian Way
7" x 9", 114 pages, two-color illustrations, $9.95 paper

Rads, Ergs, and Cheeseburgers
7" x 9", 108 pages, two-color illustrations, $13.95 paper

The Kids' Environment Book
7" x 9", 192 pages, two-color illustrations, $13.95 paper

ORDERING INFORMATION
Please check your local bookstore for our books, or call **1-800-888-7504** to order direct. All orders are shipped via UPS; see chart below to calculate your shipping charge for U.S. destinations. **No P. O. boxes please; we must have a street address to ensure delivery.** If the book you request is not available, we will hold your check until we can ship it. Foreign orders will be shipped surface rate unless otherwise requested; please enclose $3.00 for the first item and $1.00 for each additional item.

For U.S. Orders Totaling	Add
Up to $15.00	$4.25
$15.01 to $45.00	$5.25
$45.01 to $75.00	$6.25
$75.01 or more	$7.25

METHODS OF PAYMENT
Check, money order, American Express, MasterCard, or Visa. **No cash.** For credit card orders, include your card number, expiration date, and your signature, or call **1-800-888-7504**. American Express card orders can only be shipped to billing address of cardholder. Sorry, no C.O.D.'s. Residents of sunny New Mexico, add 6.25% tax to total.

Address all orders and inquiries to:
John Muir Publications
P.O. Box 613
Santa Fe, NM 87504
(505) 982-4078